DARK
IMAGES
AT SEA

DARK IMAGES

AT SEA

INTELLIGENTLY TEXTURED POETRY

Philip M. Butera

DARK IMAGES AT SEA
INTELLIGENTLY TEXTURED POETRY

Front Cover Credit: Artwork, "Mediterraneo" by Spanish artist Alex Alemany (alex@alexalemany.com, www.alexalemany.com)

Back Cover Credit: Photographed by Polish photographer Rafal Dabrowski.
Model: Patrizia Balcer (Facebook: Patrizia Fotomodel)

iUniverse books may be ordered through booksellers or by contacting:

iUniverse
1663 Liberty Drive
Bloomington, IN 47403
www.iuniverse.com
1-800-Authors (1-800-288-4677)

ISBN: 978-1-4917-8223-1 (sc)
ISBN: 978-1-4917-8222-4 (e)

Library of Congress Control Number: 2015918477

Print information available on the last page.

iUniverse rev. date: 12/14/2015

Dedicated to

Lauren Elizabeth

May your journeys bring you wonder and wisdom

Contents

Plato considered Poets empty vessels carrying both good and bad messages from Gods above and/or below. Poets needed to be watched because of their suggestive poetic power which could be used for evocative thinking and provocative behavior. Their intellectual aptitude caught somewhere between, the unknown and all-knowing; lyrical messengers of inspiration that lead men to *think*.

To *think*, to *think* - our unique purpose as humans. Poets inhabit the entirety of existence, mental, physical, internal and external searching for the word or words to describe what it is they yearn to communicate. It is essential for poets to proclaim not the story (though they have to tell it) but the essence of thought or feeling that underlies the expressive narrative. And, that intellectual articulation depends solely on the passionate psyche of the poet. How effortlessly it leaves his soul to capture an audience. The eloquent poet never forces you to imbibe but ardently invites – teasing your appetite to religiously savor. Not to swallow till completely relished. The engaged reader is appealed to continue the journey on to another word or line; his thoughts now welcoming the reverie of contemplation. The poet strives for his lyrics to resound, to mix and churn becoming one with the readers' own innermost life.

Most poets, I believe live neither in so-called reality nor in deep realms of inner awareness but in the thin ethereal stream separating the two, bridging sanity and the mysterious. Begging to take more steps into themselves yet realizing there is a line, an intellectual mark once crossed wherein art becomes absurd to those living in a predictable world. Great artists chance a glimpse to fully ignite their own imagination but elect to stay on this side of the abyss. The commitment to crossing promises the opening of many doors, however, adoration and audience appreciation are not among them. Those precious moments of pure genius come with the penalty of extreme loneliness; few are ready to permit themselves the freedom required to fully express and experience. This is equally true for the poet and his audience alike.

I love all art forms that lead us to think, dwell and linger in our minds – awakening introspection and imagination. I find it is hard to separate, art, psychology and philosophy, maybe because they all emphasize an inner attentiveness to all realms of thought, creativity and dreams.

Before I started this book of poetry, I searched my mind for a complete work about man – there may be many but I came up with two; Freud's complete works encompassing birth to death observations and Homer's - The Iliad and The Odyssey. That was it, - especially the Odyssey. It contains every element of behavior and thought, man's adventure, his journey through turbulence to find peace and embrace his love again. And then came the poetic challenge - how do you retell a perfect story that has been glorified many times?

As a surrealist poet with an existential point of view I started seeing Odysseus' adventure not as linear but a series of passages to be separated by indulgently imposing myself into the story. The Odyssey provides endless opportunities to be woven anew by my ambition as a poet armed with a palette to mix the colors of my own intellectual making. I pondered the trip from leaving Penelope to Odysseus's return 20 years later but in mixed panorama. It would be as if the winds took hold of the story at the very beginning and scattered it and the story swirled without bounds on a new landscape with a changed consistency. There they would be: Odysseus, Penelope, Circe, Calypso, the main characters against the subtext of nature and the interference of Gods. And, in homage to Homer with one thread – the sea – some would say a metaphor for life itself. But the journey of the Odyssey will take place inside my mind - without a frame only imagination. The Odyssey shall ramble against, and with, my thoughts and my thought's adventures, neurons firing creatively – as if Dali, de Chirico, Picasso and Magritte were all singular ingredient which I will then mix with Camus, Dostoyevsky and Poe, next adding Debussy, Beethoven and Vaughn Williams lastly sprinkling with Fellini.

I wanted to set the story ablaze, so while writing I listened to great classic Jazz by the legends who created it and pushed the boundaries of music. I wanted to leap over the walls I would encounter so I thought about how Charley Parker would interpret what I needed to express. I desired to find the soul of the work and interpret not the story but the magnificence of the "idea" of the story. The Odyssey lives on continually in the moment, every moment pushing that moment beyond boundaries toward the realization of perfection. Again in my mind I did not want to narrate a linear story but a destiny of mixed encounters that always possesses the totality of the story from every perspective. I would need words, photos, and artwork to express the boundlessness of Odysseus's and everyman's journey. If I were a saxophone being played by John Coltrane how would I traverse limitlessness yet be understood – not straight forward but absolutely from all perspectives at once. A glorious layered collaboration with layer upon layer of intention – unrestrained but structured, like jazz until finally the texture becomes the sea in the mind's eye, a gestalt to ignite complete imagination, the conveyance for the journey. This is an excursion, an expansion of surrealist thought pushing at the realm of awareness.

I board the ship with Odysseus. We clash at first but soon find comfort in each other. On occasion, we unite as one thought thrust into open infinity without restrictions - just traveling as an idea travels. At others times I alone am the journey seeking the realm that opens space within awareness. The scope is boundless permitting the emergence of new thoughts unhindered by margins, rolling into sequences as one transforms thought to ideas and images. Considerations spin into configurations that churn against time and reality. I become an idea, I burst into art like fireworks appearing in the sky. This idea brings promises of more ideas yet to be, yet to be interspersed with imminent ethereal imaginings. All this occurs within an open but misty forwardness in keeping with Plato's suggestion of inspiration.

Now, you as the reader have become involved leave convention behind. Do not be held back, let the veils of conviction fall away. Soar aloft and climb the horizons of your own mind – use the poems, the sentences and the words, photos and artwork to float through your own imagination. Strive to sample genius the core of great art. Find that courage and celebrate, board the thoughts you become aware of while reading and viewing. Let those thoughts couple and direct you to where they please to go. I invite you to inhabit my art to enjoy this Odyssey sweeping from antiquity weaving between my mind and yours.

Poetry Readers Comment on Philip Butera's First book of Poetry, "Mirror Images and Shards of Glass"

Philip's book is simply superb, full of fiery passion and profound insight. Although at times almost painfully difficult to digest, it compelled me to continue digging deeper into the heart of the matter. Ever elusive and evocative, this is his story. Still it seems at times addressed to me alone - an effect of genuine pathos on the reader.

"Damaged by love the wrong side up", he seems to sense a higher love. His life like a rolling stone - poisonous medications, self-destruction, sex, drugs, dread of being, and madness - appears to be an arduous journey, yet with rays of light and a longing for "a fate within faith". One may wonder how or more importantly why he has survived all the traumas and lives to tell the tales so boldly.

E

Shards brought forth the collision of my thoughts and the full damage of my mind. It openly entices the desires of the flesh that breaks the bonds of the desire of ones being, yet closes the gap of relief. It is Dante's Paradiso, Purgatorio, and Inferno. This book is an abysm of darkness, of unseemly brightness, a spew of vomit, shame, and the explosion of sperm. It is you, it is me, and it is theirs. It is all, for it is life.

R

Brilliant use of the written word. Artistic language... wrapped around seeping sadness. Fulfilled, then not. Longing for perfection of love. In search of the perfect woman who tells the truth and sees through his secret world. That appears to be a 'thread' woven through many of his poems. Provocative!

N

Insightful, beautifully written and some of the most thought provoking poetry published in recent years. Sometimes painful but somehow shrouded in hope.

D

Philip has created something that both resonates and invites the reader into his reference points; global imagery with personal touchstones. The elusive quality is what intrigues me the most. It's as though I am being engaged on an emotional/psychological plane and yet the moment my mind becomes involved in the desire to capture and define, the essence is beyond my grasp; something unidentifiable coming into focus only to lose its sharp edges and morph into something that feels not quite right. At other times, it can feel like an anvil hammering relentlessly with no indication of subsiding or mercy. Perhaps this is the disarming aspect; too vulnerable, too transparent, escape routes blocked, insistent and demanding of presence. His poetry pushes the envelope and wakens his readers to another sense not previously encountered.

L

A very enjoyable read as it was a roller coaster of emotions ranging from comedy, sexual tension, family history and his lifelong experiences...

J

This was an excellent book of poetry with a diverse subject manner ranging from the ridiculous to the utter sublime.

F

Philip is enjoying all the stages of sex, drugs and madness....throw in a little self-mutilation and the cake is baked.... fascinating and painful ride to a yet hidden"" center being." His shards of glass are always sprinkled with cocaine or dripping with blood but never leaving an obvious scar!!

K

Philip Butera; a through-the-looking-glass, writer. Rich with insightful poetic rhythm, and wonderfully meandering prose, is a spirited soul, who is sometimes lost, then reclaimed again. Such a soul---perpetually possessed with trying to find its sense of direction, while still too free of established thought to allow angst to become a barrier for attaining that euphemistic euphoria. Philip Butera remains---too restless a soul, to stop that pursuit.

L

All five star reviews for "Mirror Images and Shards of Glass" on Amazon

I would like to thank all of my collaborators. They trusted me with their creativity for my vision. This project would not have been completed without their support and faith. It was a pleasure working with such talented artists, models and photographers from around the world.

From Canada:
L. Thomson
Bonita (Bonnie) Harris

From Scotland:
Stuart McAllister
Emma Rutherford
Sarah Mua

From England:
Warwick Upton

From France:
She Nandoah
Audrey Marienkoff

From Spain:
Alex Alemany
Modesto Roldan

From Germany:
Patrizia Belcer
Jasmina Sun
Susanne Kreuschmer
Katrine Jakobsen
Jens Neubauer
Sabrina Beyer

From Poland:
Rafal Dabrowski

From Italy:
Tomaeva-Gabellini Fatima
Angelo Graziano
Giancarla Parisi
Mariano Annoni

From United States:
Kathryn Carlyle
Chantel Putman Bacon
Logan Zonas

Thank you all.

"This world is but a canvas to our imagination."
Henry David Thoreau

FROM THE EDITOR

This is a solid book of poems that exhibit a strong, unique voice; that delight in the texture of language; and that blend ancient personalities and artworks with contemporary characters and cultural concepts. The themes explored in these poems—lost love, sexuality, insanity, human nature, the purpose and effect of art, and so forth—are presented with depth and insight. Readers who seek to be challenged by language and ideas will find themselves impressed with your work. Well done.

Book One

THE ALTAR COLLAPSES

His Mind Sets Sail, Leaving His Thoughts to Guide Him

Meandering.
Set on God.
Abounding with characters.
Leaning to one side,
Then the other.
Sailing into
Darkness
Of mind.
A compulsion
To know,
To act,
To conquer.
All romantic notions
No condolences
To the dead.
They are
Patronage.
As before,
I see myself
As an idea of me—
In a conversation with myself,
About how
I have come to be
Whom I recognize
As me.
Though thoughts
Influence
My perception,
I alone
Understand
What I must do.

At night I walk on water
Never passing
What it is,
I cannot comprehend.
All these actions
To notice the
Moonlight on the seas,
Contrary to redemption.
Doubtful that I exist
In the thoughts of others,
I emote,
Hate, and wonder.
Islands produce
Mysteries, with which my mind
Empathizes,
For only beliefs, exist.
Women call.
Legs open.
The waves
Generate utterances.
They create what I cannot.
My reveries are but
Words mingled with thoughts.
Yet to understand
The reality of longing,

Ulysses watching the skies.
That is when we met:
Between a note and a dream,
Uncovering secrets.
Beyond the boundaries.

THE CAST

Written with L. Thomson

I cannot remember
A wind so harsh,
Waves so rough,
Or twilight so ineffective.

Then
I recognize the mirror
Is shattered.
And what I am
Experiencing
Is my mind
Reaching to accept
The thoughts
It produces.
Jazz infused synapses
Bursting through barriers.
In a conversation
With me,
One wherein voices
Never realize
The infinite drama.
Characters abound,
Each wishing
To be heard.
Some are beguiling;
Others at war.
Yet, from the silky
Regions of reprieve,
They appear,
Sifting
The profound

From the abstract.
And I marvel,
For they reside
Beyond art,
Beyond beauty.
Pure perfection,
They are all she.
She, always to be.
She, eternal.
She, my love.
She, reality
Appearing
In reflection.
Thoughts in collision
My fist travels through
The glass,
The mirror,
Yearning
For completion.
There is no pain
Only a journey.
I contemplate
The profound
The Odyssey.

I cannot remember
The wind so harsh,
The waves so rough,
Or twilight so ineffective.

*Artwork, "mujer de agua" by Spanish artist Alex Alemany –
e-mail: alex@alexalemany.com – www.alexalemany.com*

PENELOPE

Thirst kneels.
Hunger departs.
The sun beams.
Penelope exists.

Lips, warm;
Breasts, sweet;
Heart, heavenly
Penelope exists.

Seas lead home.
All her images
Misted in anticipation.
Penelope exists.

Call to me.
By chance,
I shall hear.
Penelope exists.

Photograph by Scottish photographer Stuart McAllister – model Emma Rutherford

CIRCE

Written with L. Thomson

Are you brave enough?
Secure enough, and
Bright enough

To know,
To grasp,
To dare,
To journey,
To trust,
To risk?

There are depths
Beneath the abyss
Where passion
Is absolute proprietor.
Desire never extinguished.
Mirrors without reflections;
Doors, no handles.
Yet beds resound—
Beds wherein lust
Chokes all logic.
A realm obsessed
Decadence,
Pleasure unleased.
Men surrender,
Yield to foraging.
Few sample her flesh.
Those who taste
Want more,
Endlessly more.

Photograph by Scottish photographer
Stuart McAllister

She is what we crave, what is
Alive in our minds,
Uncluttered energy
Raging behind emotion,

She needs no language
She is language.
Never leaving
Your mind
Never leaving.
She thrives
In your failings.
And
She detests your weakness.
Detests what is not hers
She is Circe.

CALYPSO

The prophecy foretells
Of beauty,
Delicacy, honesty,
Openness, and warmth,
Of a beautiful face
That invites,
Of breasts that pout
For affection,
Of arms that crave
To embrace,
Of legs that encircle
No other
But you,
No other
But you.
She requires only
Your love
Given freely,
Easily,
Gratefully,
Making you
A captive
Of her, of Calypso.
Persistently,
She will
Linger
In your thoughts
Till she
Is your only
Thought.

Photograph by German photographer Jasmina Sun – |
model Patrizia Balcer (Facebook Patrizia Fotomodel)

ATHENA

Written with L. Thomson

Before a compass,
Before a quest,
Eyes
Were upon us,
Directing.

A lyrical whisper
In the wind
Heads turn
Searching
Our hearts
Beckoning
Yearning for
Adventure.

She is brilliance.
Ever watchful.
Vigilant over us,
She is Athena.

Photograph by German photographer Jens Neubauer – model Sabrina Beyer

APPARITIONS

Never shy.
Her image
Carved
Into our thoughts
Bold,
Awakening,
Craving
Touch,
Left waiting,
Yearning
To be treasured,
Held,
Smothered.
Celestial.
Pure woman,
Pure art,
Painted by
Imagination
In daydreams
Coming alive.
Never quite real,
Never within reach,
Longing
Under the stars
Infinitely torment
Desire uncomplicated.
Direct
Desire, the
Incessant weakness.
Desire
The sin
To oblige.

Photograph of French Model/Artist She nandoah

TIME

Written with L. Thomson

I am
Lost
To humanity,
For
I have no need
Of humanity.

I am
Lawless
Without conformity
Without constraints
Without conformation
I will continue
Without sunrises.

I am
Forever
And always,
For
I exist.

Photograph of American Model/Artist Chantel Bacon

Endless time,
Endlessly timeless

Without conformity
Without constraints

Without conformation.

SUN

Written by L. Thomson

Perpetual movement,
Clamoured adoration,
Commanding
Obedient reverence
Yet I
Cower and shy
Perceiving
Only rage,
For there
Is nothing
Reciprocal
In this bondage.
I never established
A correct rapport.
I am the
Narcissistic
Child
Telling lies about
A God
I do not understand
And you are
Life itself,
On fire
With insistent rage
Condemning my obsession
With myself.

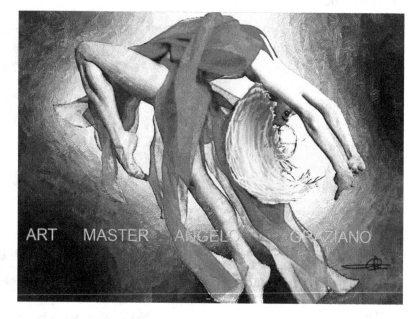

Artwork by Italian artist Angelo Graziano – model Logan Zonas

NIGHT

It is obvious,
Though
Elusive.
I walk;
She floats.
I am here;
She is everywhere.
At once,
In her presence,
Distance
Is ethereal.
My mind
Escapes reality.
My thoughts
Confront illusions
Under her spell.
Now we
In dreams long ago
Know
Contemplation
Continues
To chase an expanse.
A spellbinding
Seductress
Triumphantly
Arrives regularly
In her beguiling
Attire.
She is night.

Photograph by Scottish photographer Stuart McAllister

HOPE A LITTLE LONGER

Written with L. Thomson

It is the motion.
It is the sea.
You cling to me
In my relentless thoughts.
I howl in defeat,
But the moon,
The moon,
She whispers in mockery and
Reflects only insistence.
Come to me.
The wind is a temptress
Carrying your call.
I am lost
Without you.

It is the motion.
It is the sea.
I turn to the mirror.
The reflection
Turns away.
Rain,
Each drop, is
A cruel reminder of
My total desolation.
I search for an eternity
To be found.
Your voice is
A seam in my mind that
Creates allegories.

Photograph by Italian photographer Mariano Annoni – model & artist Giancarla Parisi

It is the motion.
It is the sea,
This claustrophobic
Place of execution.
The stars are too far away
To see my tears;
Nights, too dark
For temptation.
Moments linger.
Between thoughts,
You, in white gossamer,
Walk on water
With Jesus,
Waving good-bye.

It is the motion.
It is the sea.
When you loved me,
Were we real
Or undefined images?
Tomorrow arrived late.
Now the wounds
Bake in the sun.
I quarrel with myself
About your breasts,
Their taste, their shape.
I see no firelight,
Just expanse, just life,
Towing its consequences behind.

Artwork by Italian artist and model Giancarla Parisi

It is the motion.
It is the sea,
The impossibility of forgetting
Internal conflict
Warmed by
A sincere assumption,

Untamed and
Probing my brain—
The cancerous persistence
Of thoughts convoluted,
Wrapping around
Pokers set aflame.
Just endless emotion when
Witnessing the unknown.

It is the motion.
It is the sea.
My contemplations—
Can you hear them?
Above the waves,
Calling to you
Without a voice.
A rapport
With darkened introspection,
Always illusive.
A beautiful
Country girl,
My first reverie
Before all befores.

Photograph by Scottish photographer Stuart McAllister

It is the motion.
It is the sea,
The alone loneness, the
Absurdity of
Opaque awareness,
Mindscapes colliding
Rhythmically,
Never making sense,
Appealing to prisoners,
Undulating in redemption.
Impossible to realize,
Just sails—just sails

And distances
Undefined by the horizon.

It is the motion.
It is the sea.
It is the motion.
It is the sea.
It is the motion.
It is the sea.

When the whip
First hits my back,
The skin thinks,
Love has come.
It begs for certainty.
Then the flesh
Begins to split
As blood
Pools over the swelling.
God's laughter is heard,
Yet I know
God as pain.
It is the motion.
It is the sea.

My heart is cold.
Another sunset.
Watching nothing,
Becoming less
Blueness than blackness.
Your thighs were sweet.
I rested there.
Before the violence,
The sun
Recalled my sins.
Since then,

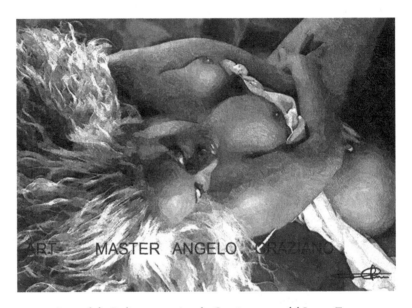

Artwork by Italian artist Angelo Graziano – model Logan Zonas

Crimson with excess,
It is the motion;
It is the sea.

Thinking
You are near,
I stare at myself.
Staring back
Then, there is you
At the tip of a thought.
Not quite another,
But one gone before
I can grasp it.
We are all
Without sanity,
Unable to comprehend.
It is the motion.
It is the sea.

I hear a cello
Crying for me
In the hands of a master
Hangman.
The sound is rude and yet comfortable,
Especially in my mind.
We divide my sight.
One of my sides is blind,
Beyond belief.
The other
Sees death
As oars row.
It is the motion.
It is the sea.

Fate deals
From a deck of jokers.
In my cabin,
A nun rests.
She is uncertain.
Rum captures my imagination.
I undress her slowly,
Savoring the crucifix
Between her naked legs.
Again, no one is there,
Just me
With a dagger.
It is the motion.
It is the sea.

A voyage
Is a remedy.
To hold thoughts
Aloft.
She told me she loved me.
When I left,
I was gone,
Simply not there,
Yet I remained
Cursed aboard
My floating, self-examining
Asylum.
It is the motion.
It is the sea.

Seeking answers, I wonder,
Am I to blame?
The war raged
Without absolution for anyone.
My mind, a voyeur,
Seceded from life.
A pale remembrance
On a lost palette,
I was summer.
Now I am
What I became:
A sailor.
It is the motion.
It is the sea.

Photograph by Scottish photographer Stuart McAllister
— model Emma Rutherford

THE STRANGER INSIDE

Written with L. Thomson

Cowardice
This current life
Cast off calendar
Shadow of days
My past
Wrapped
In miraculous saves
Bells toll
Crush mindful
Resurrections
I see me
But in shadow
Arranging seasons
No guiding light
Following
A path to the sea
The ever distance
Forlorn yet soft
Always in motion

Like deceit
Like decay

Short black skirt
Blue eyes
Your breasts
Moist
From my tears
What war was I in?
I remember shame
As limitations

Genuflected
To paradoxes
Playing cards with lives
Consequences
Transforming
Kids to corpses
No matter
Justice is
Unconscious
Eyes blinded
By anticipation

Like evil
Like extraction

Sadness
Columns in rows
I loved your embrace
As styles
Changed
We grew apart
Reveries colliding
Indifferent to emotions
You wedded
I rode the train
That never stopped
Not even
To look back
In sorrow
I cling to night
For I am elusive
Entombed in thought
Arrogant
Blemished by experience

Like stillness
Like sin

Jealous incantations
For adventures
In silk beds
With talented
Linguistic masters
They flayed
Words rhymed
With scores
Anguish and insight
Make narrow
Escapes
You on me
Then me on you
We were the moment
Haunted
By cultured reason
Those proper nouns marched
And verbs are still called
To trample plagues

Like Hate
Like Hysteria

In the dream
Within a dream
My Mother appears
I ask, "Am I in this dream"?
She asks, "Why"?
Because the distance
Is abstract and I am
No longer acting
The dream within a dream
Becoming the dream

I was dreaming
Ethereally flawed
Except
For you
Captive in dreaming
At the periphery
The sting
From the bite
Never felt

Like Assassination
Like Abstention

The choreographers
Are dead
Bombs killed their
Visions
Now dancers
Faun for Poets
Though they too
Have lost their steps
I search for you
In the wasteland
In the menacing
Thoughts
My mind
Denies me
Performance
Philosophy
Without words
Only dramatists
Searching

Like Fortitude
Like Failure

The precipice
Crumbles
Decreasing
My time
I see the turbulence
The Ocean
Demanding
I dissect
The metaphor
From the allegories
Mist from waves
Caresses my flesh
Impersonating
Your tongue
Rehearsing
Insanity for a living
I fall again
From the cross
Into your arms

Like Stealing
Like Strangling

The sign
After death
Says welcome
I enter a room
Of mystery and mirrors
She appears
While every
Image of me
At every age
Parallels
Moments of time
All reflections

Form
An idealized me
That is now her
She kisses my lips
"You are me"? I ask
She replies, "No,
I am you".

Like Noumenon
Like Nonsense

And I, again
Board the ship.

Photograph by German photographer Jens Neubauer

WATERY INTERLUDE

Gathering
Black clouds
Bundle,
Choking
The last,
Slender threads
Of pale light
On the dank,
Battered
Break wall
Behind me.

Maddened,
Harsh winds
Sourly whip
The churning lake,
Bandying
Colorless droplets
Into the gray,
Glistening mist,
Glazing my face
With a coarse mask
Of burrowing sand.

Photograph by Scottish photographer Stuart McAllister

Racing
Cold waves
Break against me.
They are bleeding
White curls
Of madness born
To smash
What is concrete,
Erasing knowledge.
My steps continue
Toward oblivion.

Hearing
Seagulls screeching—
Optical jargon—
I see everything
Swept away,
The water
Weighing down
The pull and the push.
My thoughts are perceptual,
Forward, moving
Down into distance.

Angels are
Lost in a world
Of pain
In lover's arms,
Unloved.
Storm of the heart
Bringing to mind
Tortured betrayal,
Lightening torrents,
Dark encounters,
Blurred apparitions.

Rushing
Gestures caress me,
Striking a strange euphoria.
Uninterrupted succession.
Umbilical reconnections.
Opera dreaming.
Recurring déjà vu.
A loving surrender.
The dramatic voyage.
No longer inquisitive;
Merely redundant.

Spiraling,
Impossible reasoning.
Illusions of existence.
Brutalized
Rocks jostling.
Sounds unformulated.
Abandoning consciousness.
Naive inevitability.
Directionless.
No intervening space.
Watery images.

Beginnings.
Questioning a Divine.
Liquid-infused association.
Neurochemical schizophrenia.
Inhibitory disconnections.
Disguisable edges.
Transcending
Emphasized conflicts,
Memories, or exhibitions.
Vertically arranged horizons.
Musical assertions.

Existing within.
The absurdity
Of my life
As a paintbrush,
Out past beyond
Composing color,
Layers unfolding.
What is realized?
A solitary figure
Contemplating sanity
Through madness.

Photograph by Canadian photographer Bonita (Bonnie) Harris

I Encountered Myself as a Framed Thought in a Maritime Museum

She is a joyous opera.
Angelic voices surround her.
Her strength is legendary.
In our kisses is the sweetest recognition of life.
I behold her, tanned and in splendor, at the shore,
Each of her breasts heavy with pity for those who will never taste them.
The island is lush,
Or so I thought
I awake in a bed with women, women surrounding me,
Their bodies all about me,
Catering to me.
They never speak.
Their eyes are deep blue;
Their hair, soft and buttery.
Sex for them is familiar.
Different women join
I never left our windowless room.
When I slept, I was still awake.
The women snuggled against me.
I drank sweet-tasting wine.
My own voice was all I heard.
The women seemed to float silently.
I bathed in exotic flowers.
My hair never grew.
My body never seemed stronger
But, with all of this,
I remained plagued.
Am I joyous or condemned?
This room without an exit
The women gently pressing against me.
They interlaced to become a living dream.

I awoke one day and felt as if a tropical wave were embracing me.

My eyes searched, one face then another..

All were identical,

Every face was her face, the ideal face.

I brought myself to myself and closed my eyes tight, very tight.

I had no thoughts, just an intimation that Athena was watching.

When I opened my eyes I was in a small, white room and strapped to a table.

A door opened. Fantazius Mallare, Joe Bonham, and George Harvey Bone entered.

I tried to shout, but my voice was lost.

The men passed through me to the other side of my thoughts.

Then she, she smiled. It was she, so very beautiful.

There was tubing placed into my arms,

Electrodes taped to my head,

Wires inserted into my ears.

There was a large, oval light overhead.

I sensed others around me.

She said, "I will love you till reality and abstraction are one."

A saw began to cut.

Poe sat beside me.

Auden is writing a libretto about pain.

Past lovers collect my aspirations

Trapped in what is already, I fall through my thoughts.

A beatific nun undresses for me.

She is warm and creamy, delicate and intense.

Performing through her image, *the* beautiful, blonde-haired woman appears.

She is complete.

I experience her, but I know she is not present.

Yet the ideal of her remains.

Or am I the ideal in another's thought?

Words, thoughts perform without significance.

Soon the references to existence disappear

Illusions inside, delusions inside. Imagination inside—images of imaged imaginations.

Smirking, she says, "I am Circe and you are past madness—for now."

Rethinking thinking, I come to what was, arriving from what may be.

I contemplated a way back to sanity,

A journey through the magic theater's maze.

Literature is always the source.

Beyond solutions in order to arrive before any questions are asked.

Circe's lips tease my thighs.

Am I here, or is that me at the back of her thoughts?

Dali and I sail on butterscotch clouds.

In the lull between moments,

There is Brahms piano concerto.

Many summers pass.

Existing is pure fantasy now.

Animals appear, but as phenomena, not knowledge.

Truth leads me to the fringe of what has no center.

As actors, we are always incognito.

Being me - I recall that the last commandment is about forgiveness.

Circe feeds me her nipple.

I am committed in the face of what I cannot grasp.

Relentless, I stay attached to her breast,

Sublime, I see myself on the other breast, enjoying what angels reveal about idyllic exquisiteness.

Ulysses, in a black mask, addresses me in the past tense as I walk among the future dead.

Bells chime madly.

I know it is time to retrieve myself.

Eurymachus hands me a note about Penelope's making love to Antinous.

Polyphemus throws a boulder through a stained-glass cathedral window.

I catch a shard, a thought.

It bloodies my hand.

I squeeze it until Helen's name ruminates in my mind's eye.

She wears a short black cocktail dress

Men crawl to her

While Paris chases mirror images

Nymphs have inclinations about me.

From behind an arm quickly comes across and cuts my throat.

My thoughts take route to destiny.

Heaven is just another café outside the realm of believing.

God is on vacation, so Cleopatra comes to my defense.

She says, "Never give up on what it paradoxical."

Reveries open apertures in order to collect scenarios.
The ocean is an heirloom,
A casualty, an insistence and an invitation.
I dig into my thoughts.
My crimes perpetrating time.
Doomsday ensembles
Play jazz from where pleasure resides.
Wishes greet me.
Saints and virgins, naive from inquiries,
Insist that they only exist in my mind
I have no reason left, only consequences.
Ethereal influences
Rush down from colliding clouds
These commotions I must now reside among
Till infinity has a sailors cadence
To where the end begins:
Deep out to sea
Amid myths.
So, following the stars,
I comprehend
The problems of: Sleep and dreams
In the nightmares
That inhabit
The realms
We devote to thinking.
I open the map,
How
Remarkable
Astonishment
Can be
In the light,
In the dark,
On the sea.

Artwork by Spanish artist Modesto Roldan

In the tumbling
Beyond what lasts
There is art.

In my hand was a single shard of mirror.
I comprehended the divine order of my journey.
I have drowned many times,
Yet I remain the character I resurrect
When blood spills
And love is an influence

Artwork by French artist Audrey Marienkoff

THE DEATH OF DISAPPEARANCE

Annabel Lee
Set up her easel
Inside the blaze of Vesuvius.
Asylum angels
Mixed the paints
On her palette.
"Misty," being played
I passed among the flames
To serve Limoncello
Gauguin told me that
Van Gogh was gone.
"Gone where", I said
He pointed away
For choice is a mental state.
We spin
On a world, that blends our thoughts

Artwork by Russian/Italian artist Tomaeva-Gabellini Fatima

      Dead characters
      Looking for their creators
      Swore they would
      Never die again.
      They admitted.
      The lush life
      Is physical
      Marie Antoinette
      Loved my laugh.
      I stripped her.
      D'Artagnan advised me
      Passion
      Is like being
      Dressed for murder
      Carrying only a thought
      Walking into a Bohemian Café

Pirates court barmaids
In the royal brothel.
The explorers,
Dressed in drag,
Chased us to the brink
How insane to meet
Myself there
When I was naked
And comfortable
With Calypso.
The cattails
Struck my back
Leaving reminders
There are no sanctuaries.
Only tattooed women
With legs that uncross

    I found
    A weathervane
    Disguised as romance
    Slumbering against
    My opened mind
    Desire sailed about
    My thoughts
    Laughing before dying
    I lead myself
    To past me.
    The sea rolls illusions over the horizon,
    Demons permeate my mind?
    With strength and love
    My will shatters
    Prayers only bring rain
    I dance with memories.

Lost in dreams
Rising above damage,
Athena wakes me.
I smile
From a canvas
Raskolnikov places his arm under my head.
Ulysses simply asks, "Who is your Penelope?"
My heart is a false impression
Every poet
Knows what Plato preached
As Aristotle died
I say, "I don't believe in boundaries."
I followed anonymous women
The treasure I did not
Appreciate is
Happiness.

Erotic drawings are etched
From dreams
Past those who I once loved
In banquet bedrooms
Hammers pound
Axes are sharpened
I step forward
To the front of my mind
Where the trial has begun
I am my first witness
But I have no defense
Only an aesthetic inclination
Rapture sweeps the jury
In the wake
I am condemned to find
What it is I am after

Alone inside myself
Unchained and restored
Once and evermore,
I see a last vision
Of my reality:
It is you,
Naked and pleased,
In honeyed acceptance.
Yet you look away
Toward the charisma
Of the waves
Each leaving a message
Reminding you
Of my death again
And again
However, I am not dead

    Annabel Lee was
    Setting up her easel
    In the blaze of Vesuvius.
    Asylum angels
    Were
    Mixing the paints
    On her palette

Photograph by Scottish photographer Stuart McAllister

EXEMPLARY FAILURE

At the outsiders' Rejection Hotel,
The rooms are long and narrow like coffins.
The walls are tapestries of silk death shrouds.
The windows are like every heart: blackened.
The doors have no hinges, no exits or entrances.
The time is always when it began
Because the pain never ends.

All the rooms are heated very warm, almost hot.
I am on the twentieth floor, sweating.
I slowly walk the steps to the basement
The furnace flames are silver-white-yellow tinged with blue.
The day lingers in a mortician's dream.
Buried alive in thought- controlled suffocation,
No one ever dies. They just wait for the redemption that will never approach.

There are no exits here. It is best to punish oneself from the start
Self-inflicting a beheading in the lobby, where the living lap up the betrayals,
The teary-eyed onlookers wishing they could hang from a high tree.
I have found the engine room. My father looks at me.
With disgust, he tells me to strip.
The cold-eyed women I have made love to in cathedral pews wave to me.
The red glowing branding iron is pressed into my chest.

The children's merry-go-round is spinning, spinning out of control.
Cheating ghosts of girlfriends' past burn my soul with lies.
Thoughts copulate with antecedent overtures, dancing in tempests.
The iron sears my hands together—only fair for a thief who steals happiness.
Mary and my mother are in a cage, restrained from knowing.
The priests line up to rape my enthusiasm as my father invites prostitutes.
My hair burns. My face is fire-glazed with melting glass.

At the hospital, Jason and his men ask if I am comfortable.
The medics are applying ammonia and sanding my wounds.
My mouth fills with liquid lye; my eyes bathe in steam.
Pain is a dangerous and potentially deadly ongoing process
Christianity knows that functions steeped in agony find meaning not reasoning.
I moan and point to vulture-angels floating in a rum cake racing past gazelles.
A needle pumps pleasure drugs into my system so the hurt can paradoxically survive.

I think she is blonde, the woman sewing my chest together.
Smiling, she asks if my stay has been pleasant and rewarding.
The uncreative collide easily and swish down the bloodied drain.
Emptied of assurance, Ulysses is noticed through the eyes of Hersent.
The quartermaster famous for sublime androgyny takes the ship farther out.
I say, I just need a scalpel, a map, and a dream to disappear from this canvas.
Seamen laugh and stab each other with ice picks until all are irrelevant.

Slitting my wrists, I became the echo of recollections I have never seen.
In the afterglow when the wasteland spoke I fulfilled the metamorphose.
Sitting on barstools and wearing turtlenecks, the demons ask about forgiveness
Lonely and without any memories, I use a straight razor to account for my sins.
Toll barriers immediately surround me summoning me for my existential thoughts.
Circe undresses and squats on my face, rubbing and riding me to nourish her pleasure.
Unable to see my reflection in the night, I become everything unfamiliar to me.

Philosophy captains come to my bed with bawdy nuns and offer me solutions.
Crime scene detectives ask if I have any idea of how or when I was murdered.
A girl from Michigan hisses, in my direction. Her nipples arrest my endeavors.
With my sailor suit in tatters, and my mind delinquent I fly into a Barrie novel.
Chronological arrangements of my sins begin to appear on the cold-blooded clouds.
With a bluesy twang, I sing "Sweet Sixteen" as the Trojans rip my flesh.
Women are raped after seeing me in a holographic image of them doing the raping.

I drink tequila and venture out to meet the Anglicans who hold my thoughts for ransom.
Attack-enthusiasts dreaming about the considerations of a flat earth sharpen their knives.
As the victim of my loneliness, I crawl into the forest where Alice dared not to venture.
The maître d' asks if I want to have my mind served on a torture driven Reformation table.

Like a rebel at the eclipse of time between gentry and salvation, I decompose into myself.
The world outside my window is a color frieze of drab tomorrows and uncreative egos.
Stained with absent reflections, I search the backwoods for a maimed goddess to love.

At last, I can see my images, my images in heroic schizophrenia, lacking any benefit.
"Superfluous," you shout when your stone is the first to draw my blood.
Cruel and perverse disappearing hallucinations shape realizations in your portrayals.
My consciousness lapses from lonesome to ambiguous, which means I am no longer.
Together, all the sacrificed characters who lived through insanity are found weeping.
Music plays, bombs explode, and I, with Sicilian charm, address the girl on a swing.
Bullets hit my face and I disappear behind a wounded breast that leaks enlightenment

It all feels purifying, the exploding pieces of me flying apart—my destiny like love lost.
As was surmised, I do not exit. I am killed many times by my own hand.
Communion is served but conclusions have been substituted for any reality.
The black doctor rams a spiked steel rod down my throat.
My psychologist spreads her long legs to the saints while asking God for redemption.
Veterans with posttraumatic stress disorder are mashed in cauldrons, becoming archivists.
Anal probes separate imaginative anthologies from lackluster American thinking.

Fixed on your breasts, Polyphemus comes to the hidden door to bury himself in antidotes.
Belladonna and diamonds are served with aspic chocolate so that death will be horror-filled.
In the alley, natives are rolling confusion into the disappearing fields of forgotten time.
In Palermo during the war, all women were nuns, because whores were common.
I search the forbidden island, Aeaea, located at the edges of the world to find you.
Meanwhile, at the gravesite where all the I's I've become are in line to meet me.
You arrive and keep me in a waxed form until I experience the hatchet burrowing in my face.

Maxx left with his dog friends, back to the big bang to become apostolic with madams.
On the horizon, my smile caught a bullet and pure acid splashed in my bath.
Now I want to say I am sorry, but the baffling memories only roll upon themselves.
Whipped incessantly, I drag myself to where Pilate pisses and drips before washing.
You look through my eyes into yours to see how liquids flow down your legs
Lacking in genius, the crowd makes me the scapegoat for the slave trade.
After sex, you check my shackles while displaying your spread legs to the drunks.

God welcomes me into the room and introduces me to his inner circle of confidants.
I take a chair across from Hitler and Lincoln, who are holding hands and smiling at Jesus.
Caligula wants to make love, but God knocks him away with an ornamented Milky Way cane.
Cards are dealt. They disappear to become constellations. Our eyes turn inward.
We make up hands according to the thousands more people we need to murder.
We play for eternity; the winner destroys humanity in the most deplorable ways.
Surrealist artists in existential dreams try to career into dark images, but Nixon stabs them.

As I show my cards, my feet are nailed to the floor. Funeral music plays.
Timing is only a creative misreading suspended outside the recalcitrant sieve of unbelievers.
God points to me. She says shyly, "You are lost. The executioner waits."
I drift away from my thoughts, traveling backward to land without thoughts.
In a foxhole where my childhood house once stood, I embrace the illusions patrolling my mind.
When the rehearsal war is over, the singing admiral forces me to swallow apparitions.
The acting coach tells me I cannot even act the part of myself.

The loneliness of living inside thoughts created by my images, dulls me.
I have always been an outcast. My tears are singed with ambiguity and futile love.
The sky showers warm sunshine on the breasts that surround me.
Hooks of meanings disassemble as weapons fail to consecrate any conversations.
Walking with prophets, a beautiful, longhaired, artist catches my eye.
She says her name is Eve and that she is giving away golden apples. I ask for one.
When I climax, she screams for Zeus and all existence continues on a falsehood.

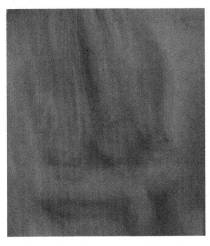

Photograph by Scottish photographer Stuart McAllister

SAILORS BENEATH A CRUMBLING BRIDGE AT TWILIGHT

This metaphor is innocent.
Remove your mask.
A brain but no mind.
A body but no heart.
Frankenstein is our father.
He is lingering on water,
Twisting sobriety.
You will remain naked.
I will always be in danger.
Sailors are meticulous artists.
Moonlight and a sextant:
Misfortune carried as cargo.
The gods listening to Mingus.

Hanging above the mast,
Imagining yourself dead
And conversations alive,
You leave the canvas.
I am never complete.
The ocean roars:
Ardent passion
And abject murder.
Me inside of you,
Disappearing further,
Never transforming
Images of spectral conceit.
The gods listening to Coltrane.

Photograph by Scottish photographer Stuart McAllister

A dagger at your throat.
My personality on a spit.
Romancing irresponsibly
The anatomy lesson.
False turns in tragedies.
Nails lengthened.
Choirs of serpents.
Footsteps arriving.
Uncomfortable in my skin.
Decorative incentives.
Ctimene in cold waves.
Sunbathing remembrances.
The gods listening to Miles.

Strapped in,
Weighted down.
Gutted of fullness.
Alter-ego mirrors
Without a guide.
Our minds distorted.
Seagulls hunting.
Exquisite indoctrination.
Clouds over floating bodies.
Recoloring the black death.
Monastic explorers.
Terror always surviving.
The gods listening to Barbieri.

Life perseveres.
Your stomach cut open.
Me like a windmill.
The flaying is real.
You knowing.
I simply rehearsing.
Blasphemous contradictions.
Sharpened garden tools.

Bipolar analogies.
Handcuffed to banal negations.
Disappearing visions—
Just belladonna dreams.
The gods listening to Burrell.

Thirst and vinegar.
Prodding masochists.
Swords unsheathed.
Roses on your casket.
Our passionate seduction.
Furrows on my forehead.
Shimmering scalpel blades.
Bones breaking.
Complex interactions.
Drinking from bedpans.
You riding me to finish.
Mannequins fishing for strangers.
The gods listening to Brubeck.

How much can be tolerated?
Hecuba knowing that Astyanax will die.
Nine sites of Troy proclaimed jazz-free.
The arrogance of stealing a wife.
Looking at the aftermath of misery.
The gold on ships.
Helen nude in the shower.
Andromache on stage
Children murdered.
The face of beauty prevails.
Lies and misfortune shape happiness.
When a woman tames a man.
The gods listening to Silver.

Scalding accusations,
Urinal aspirations
Making love in mind,
A smirk of kindness.
The ship shattering.
Hands in orifices.
Slumber beyond mathematics.
Switchblade jabs.
Reason to cry.
Waiting for land or admiration.
Circumstantial tributes.
You naked on a cross.
The gods listening to Hawkins.

Sorcerers pretending.
Pain never ending.
The broad daylight
Burning holes
Through indifference.
Your hysterics
Marveling at the unseen.
Lashed to rowing oars.
Using your appetite,
Disclosing all ambition.
Spears on treadmills.
Rewarding mysteries.
The gods listening to Parker.

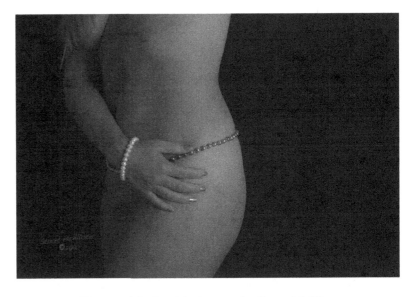

Photograph by Scottish photographer Stuart McAllister

Sexual intoxications.
Ships without enlightenment.
Abstract thinkers surrealizing.
Insects in our blood.
Terror in our blinded eyes.
Fear yet to be overcome.
Every nightmare revisited.
Sailors frightening tempests.

That smile between your legs.
Consciousness, loss of ambition.
Transparent suffering from dreaming.
Those hanging from braids of glass.
The gods listening to Monk.

In cold reality,
The drill drilling deeper,
The brakes failing.
Scissors cut.
Interiors collapse.
You declare your innocence,
Listening obliquely
To the beat of your heart
In my hands,
Disappearing deeper,
Abandoning reality.
Climbing breasts to reach towers.
The gods listening to Gillespie.

Exits to enter.
Stillborn executioners
Yet to commit sins,
Awaiting punishment.
Stigmata of your own making.
Ensemble scars opening.
Necrophilia-related turbulence.
Hurting from time.
Stay calm, but weep
Your corpus callosum severed.
Thoughts cannot decipher
Syntactical deception.
The gods listening to Rollins.

Treacherous bacteria
Overcoming death,
Bleeding as you sigh.
Anvils pounding.
Matches igniting.
Judged by Zeus.
Exclamations of persuasion.
Ithaca inconsolable.
Helen reading André Breton.
You and Circe preferring conflict.
Animistic sexual inferences.
My lonely separation from the waves.
The gods listening to Jobim.

Encountering transformation.
Desires beyond despair.
Time sickly and dull.
Break-wall intermissions,
Tumbling interludes.
Needles injected.
Knowledge digesting.
Slumbering into death.
Enchanted ruffians.
Lips curled with tacks.
Deceiving the last exception.
Blood dripping feverishly.
The gods listening to Hubbard.

Forge instruments,
A glow with flames.
An experience for you.
A dagger stabbing.
Hector falling.
Achilles felled by egotism.
Prophets painting abstractions.
Plato condemning poets.

Discordant confidantes.
Cardiac propaganda.
Revisionists bowing to Calypso.
Conflict waiting for a country.
The gods listening to Kirk.

Junkies in leather.
Inspirational liberation.
Anal appetites.
Delirium clawing at you.
Spiked dilemmas.
Deep-sleep hallucinations;
Wide-awake phenomenon.
Dunkirk, Da Nang, and Iwo Jima.
Drunken sailors,
Baptized but insane.
The romantics have arrived,
Cleaning turmoil from childhood.
The gods listening to Adderley.

You beg for forgiveness.
Dali's Last Masturbator arrives.
Moulin Rouge illusionists.
My mind poisoned with thinking.
Night approaching.
Troy in disorder.
Menelaus at a funeral.
Fénelon tells a tale.
Torrid syncopation
You promised to me.
Sexual psychiatry
Opening like an umbrella.
The gods listening to Hampton.

Photograph by Scottish photographer
Stuart McAllister– model Sarah Mua

Alone,
Beneath the wheel,
Repenting, and
Squandering promises,
I remain uncaring.
Priests with searching fingers.
Aristotle reading Euripides.
Parlayed incestuous suitors.
Ships commanded by resurrected art.
Experiencing fear.
Arousing the daughters of Agamemnon.
Cannonballs across the bow.
The gods listening to Getz.

Culmination manifestos.
Expectation analysis.
Whipped unmercifully,
Wishing to win.
Insanity pervading.
Scarcity of thought.
Removing all sums
Outside the historical.
Desdemona on her knees.
Crusade casualties.
Me conspiring with Iago.
Shakespearean melodrama.
The gods listening to Turrentine.

Arrogant performers.
Irritating dreamers.
An undertone of loneliness.
Rabid dogs recovering.
The sweaty blacksmith.
Breasts heavy with crème.
Flames screaming.
Acid sparks dappling.

Amorphous, mechanistic love.
Incomprehensible trampling.
The cigarette burns in ceremonial motion.
Confusion stubbornly dismissed.
The gods listening to Carter.

Brain disturbances.
Precarious insurrection.
Liquid tombstones.
Poetry surrendering.
Revenge being just
My self-hatred.
You, on the contrary:
Ignorant indictments.
The Silk Road opening.
Watery innuendos
Writhing with penetration.
Dysfunctional molecules.
The gods listening to Hancock.

Pigs going to slaughter.
The pendulum swinging.
Heartbeats rushing.
Memories destroyed.
Razors exercising.
Perpetual gears grinding.
Curare-speckled spirits.
Knives in luster.
Madness abounding.
Cactus spankings.
Distasteful prey,
But always the blood.
The gods listening to Sanborn.

Howl.
Reading about Dean Moriarty.
Rigged sails.
The deaf pretending;
Blind heroes with pitchforks.
Metaphysical aphrodisiacs.
Corkscrew depression.
Death hallucinations.
Choreographers in purgatory,
Harmonizing with the Devil.
We remain entwined,
Clamoring for an indictment.
The gods listening to Jones.

The screams—inevitable.
Disappearing in destiny.
Blistered faces.
Icons dismantling.
Abhorrent ethereality.
Paranoiac objections.
Spiteful torments.
Phoenix persuading Pyrrhus.
This train without a conductor.
Picasso meeting Braque.
Laocoön against the house.
Your unabated sexual appetite.
The gods listening to Mulligan.

Fists pounding,
Scars opening,
Blood dripping.
Schizophrenic sirens.
Earwax conspiracies.
Despicable internal wrath.
Resurrecting annihilation.
Eurymachus making his move.

Artwork by French artist Audrey Marienkoff

Swooning discourse.
Detesting heroines.
Weathermen in heaven
Brazenly intoxicated.
The gods listening to Shorter.

Bleached horizons.
Ricochet bolos.
Meticulous grating.
Cocaine lamentation.
Gyrating with agony,
I have forgotten you.
Deliverance from a malady.
Predictions from warriors.
Clever warnings
From Jack the Ripper.
Unthinkable tempests.
Five years on one breast.
The gods listening to Desmond.

Extreme combustion.
Devouring yourself,
Fixated on becoming
Stretched parallels.
Wine-drinking carelessness.
Pins and oblivion.
Engendered thighs.
Preliminary upheavals.
Melting face lacerations.
Frenzied turbulence.
Liquid nausea.
Hammers resounding.
The gods listening to Sandoval.

Stalked by Dante.
The symbolist inspired,
Interjecting ice picks.
The palladium defiled.
Demodokos singing
No rules,
Just extinction.
Slaughtered antagonists.
The insects crawling.
Legends blinded.
Dead mothers for sale.
Nobody caring.
The gods listening to Pastorius.

Needy, wanting medications.
Damnation in announcements.
Singing "Ave Maria."
Spiny recompense.
Stab deep,
Deeper.
Excessive diminishment.
Glass ground into faces.
No regard.
Cancer cells.
Divine theories.
Infected reasoning.
The gods listening to Tatum.

Everlasting
Rings of blood.
Waterhouse looking for subjects
The bullets penetrating,
Harder, harder, harder.
Doctors with probes.
Beautiful oblivion.
Branding your chest,

Artwork by Italian artist Angelo Graziano – model Logan Zonas

You searching for corpses.
I no longer exist.
Lady Macbeth sleepwalking.
Inevitable war casualties.
The gods listening to Grappelli.

Straps across backs.
Greeks in horse carts.
Women raped at the Phaeacian court.
Lessons in protocol delivered
For stealing beautiful queens.
The spirit of Tiresias is transitory.
Eva Braun posing for Glamour Shots.
Realms where reason goes away.
Troy burns, as does Detroit.
Motorcade wives and deserted children.
Philosophical theories about death.
Calvert knowing the density of deceit.
The gods listening to Ferguson.

Menelaus the instigator.
Wild Cassandra disappearing.
Cyrus sending clay ships.
The royal wedding.
Numbing you,
Infecting you,
Desiring you.
How absurd.
There is nothing left of you,
Just pure hatred for my existence,
Your thoughts focusing.
You will never forget me.
The gods listening to Reinhardt.

Artists remake beauty
Without torment and emotion.
Voluptuous yet unattainable,
A marvel without regret.
Free to go
To the prison of expressions,
You will never comprehend
The revulsion around you.
Yet the ship travels toward dawn.
Commiserating bravado,
Briseis, Tecmessa, and Chryseis in their beds.
Fractious deception.
The gods listening to Allison.

Imagists Paris and Helen.
The former killed by Philoctetes,
Rejected by Oenone.
The latter confronting me,
Her nude body trembling.
Atop the dead bodies, we claw at each other,
Hungry for what will come next.
My mouth frothing with incomprehension.
She standing, bending, spreading, and forgetting.
The axe severing my head.
Rumors about Nausicaa.
The caprice of perfect ideas.
The gods listening to Jamal.

Self-insolence.
After-the-fact winnings.
Commands of coverage.
Forgetting the tribute to Masson.
Slippery encounters. Conditional similarity.
Provisions for misfits.
Eternal ménage à trois.
Unfiltered through cubist surrealism.

Photograph by Scottish photographer Stuart McAllister

Atlantis lost in a poker game.
Revelations about the unthinkable.
Conscious imagination traveling.
Gloomy compositions confront Argos.
The gods listening to Montgomery.

Sailors are dead.
Demons of the soul.
Unsavory obsessions.
The quest for understanding.
The son of Hector buried.
A knife for scrimshaw.
Jazz becoming the intrigue.
Sinister relations plundering.
Ithaca soon to be wakened.
Crimes with dubious equations.
Greeks colorizing simplicity.
Shameless convert buccaneers.
The gods listening to Peterson.

Too much silver and gold.
Victors monotonous in their greed.
Carved diversions depict indemnity.
Grandstand death.
Aristotle's theoretical life.
Pessimism, the two-toned finality.
Sailing extended into theatrics.
My legs around your neck.
The Golden Fleece hanging.
Language dismissing Amazons.
Cultural chandeliers expressing outrage.
Innumerable consolations trampled.
The gods listening to Gordon.

Domestic discord.
Death lengthening.
Unavoidable carcasses.
Women begging for twists to kill.
Napoleon perfecting genius.
Priam refusing the alternative.
Vultures and sunshine striking.
Neptune negotiating contracts in Italy.
Aeneas escaping his dual personality.
When your eyes closed,
You found me to the right of Frost.
Someone shouted, "I am no one."
The gods listening to Sanders.

Very cunning,
Turning time around.
Spectators from the past
Distinguishing between
Delusion and caprice.
Calypso's retort.
Hermes questioning motives.
A bag of wind.
Methodological forgiveness.
Interval, tone, and rhythm.
The lightness of beauty
Witnessing my reversal.
The gods listening to Kenton.

Death knell.
Strip searches.
Athena in magnificence.
Without gods,
Humankind is nothing.
Vomiting in coarse reality,
I proclaim,
"Pure thought excludes deities."

Bloodless
And without cost,
Strangers die as frauds.
Existentialists emerge.
The gods listening to Armstrong.

An island.
A memory.
Waves splashing.
Rocks disappearing.
Weddings planned.
Turbulent transfiguration.
Thought.
Time never stopping to move.
Dissolved in mesmerist thievery.
Converging ten years into twenty.
Listening to what defies listening.
Gripping the intellect.
The gods listening to Hendrix.

The metaphor is dead;
Life, ambiguous.
Fear compelled you to find me,
But you were never flesh.
Reflect away now.
The id dismantled.
Mashed incentives.
Pitiless ambitions.
Yin–Yang bandits.
Impressionistic expressionists.
Modern antiquity.
Contours without edges.
The gods listening to Debussy.

Temple injustice.
Suicide incompetence.
Navigating for Calypso;
Desiring Circe.
The mind escaping.
Athena above, elevating,
Thoughts unbound,
Penelope and Telemachus sighing.
Behind the scenes,
Suitors sharpen swords.
Very arrogantly,
I write poetry.
The gods listen.

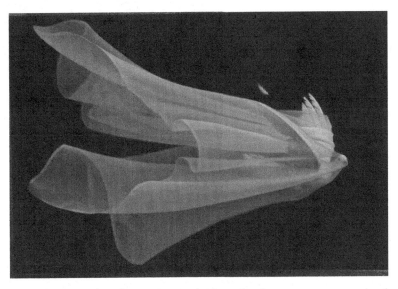

Artwork by Spanish artist Alex Alemany – e-mail: alex@alexalemany.com – www.alexalemany.com

THE LADY'S REPLY

Written with L. Thomson

Inside her locket,
A purge
Or a rebuttal.
Catacombs for Impressionists
Mimicking the sarcophagus of chastity
For the quiescent masses,
Hearing only the voracious moodiness
Of the sea,
The surly indifference
Of the sea.

Thunderous waves in unrepentant assault.
Shadowing screams of a thousand souls,
Endless and enduring.
Slicing a glimpse
Too fleeting to capture.
Those wishes crashing on the shore.
The moist spray.
Your sweet lips trembling.
The waves insist
I stay unclothed,

Artwork by French artist Audrey Marienkoff

Unprotected.
A sign from Neptune.
Shall I be his mistress?
Whose lover shall I be?
What shall I be?
Shards and splinters

Cut deeply,
Yet I am aware of my aching mind.
A character within my recollections.
Searching for explainable exits.

A concerto of thought against images.
Heaven plays host to rippling mysteries.
Connected to every expanse,
We are a curious experience,
Enabled by exhibition,
Grounded by encounters.
Insomnia is the sea's source of genius.
What color is water?
What color is doubt?
My bare figure,

Naked and alive,
Soft and smooth,
Silhouetted by innuendo.
Aware of romance that abolishes myth.
My thighs against your mouth.
Gossamer phantoms appear.
As we descend, you whisper, "Love me."
We are a strange surrealism,
My virginity dispatching the balletomane,
Another carnival whore lost to possibilities

Bound by too small, shiny, red shoes
Clicking in desperate hope.
No looking glass to correct distortion.
Once again, I see
What revelatory measure eliminates.
My beautiful breasts are heavy to your touch.
Fireflies collect in bottles.
They, like you, have libertine eyes,

Peering with determined calculation
From intimacy to duration.

Our oneness tightly entwined:
An abacus without reminiscences
Poetic nocturnal purity.
Why must dreams and love
Always obey the shyness of the moon?
A crated beauty murmurs.
I am not the answer;
I am not the solution.
I am the night's analyst
Taking precarious backstrokes.

Scripted applause dwindles.
There is urgency in anguish,
This net pulls tight,
Tighter.
You see me exposed
Once more,
Ethereally woven between designs.
Joyous once more,
The waves gather anew.
What stories do they hold secret?

Photograph by Scottish photographer Stuart McAllister

These waves rush nowhere,
Discovering you and me
Stalled in stained-glass moments.
There is wisdom in slumber,
Spewing virtue
Like oozing magma,
A river of deception—
Contemporary Styx.
On the prowl,
I am no guide,

No hero,
No sage.
Just a poet.
Just a shoreline.
Anthologies of color
Show hapless desolation.
Toulouse by the river.
Degas eyes dancers.
Monet strokes his palette knife.
Gauguin eats voluptuous breadfruit

Dripping from fame
Picasso paints
Personal pejoratives.
Ethereal imagery
Transcends Dali's legend.
The elongated limbs
Are Modigliani's humor.
And
Vincent continues
To continue.

As I innocently weep
Beside him.
Words, whorl at me.
Sylvia wears her angst,
Her shield of tormented armor,
Defying the truth as her own.
Wallace ponders his clavier
We are consumed by the hunt.
The white whale.
Is an apparition for all.

Simpered platitudes,
Obsequious offerings,
Reconstituted remembrances.

José casts beyond the beauty of the rose
To the unforgiving landscape.
I promise myself to the sea.
Lovers once
Winnowed by time.
Erosion of the soul,
Tumbling and turning.

The albatross's reflection
Undulating while being considered.
Longing for pleasure.
Longing for intimacy.
Longing for the sea
To rush and cleanse.
All those waves continue
Like enlightened thoughts.
White, curling foam:
Always gone before remembered.

Seize my love.
Use me.
Read me.
Paint me as
Unholy and redemptive,
Swirling in distress.
You, my heart.
Me, your soul.
Both for the taking.
The unkind chill

I rub Aladdin's lamp
Allowing night to steal from day.
Rational thinking prevails.
Adoration is a solitary craft,
A sail requesting wind.
Bound eternally in a dance of chaos,

I untie the phantoms.
You toss over a life raft.
The anchor bids farewell,
Circe and Calypso embrace.

Photograph by German photographer Jens Neubauer – model Sabrina Beyer

THE ENIGMA OF TWO SOULS PLAYING CHESS WITH THEIR MIRROR IMAGES

Stars collide,
But not in my lifetime.
Solar systems collide,
But not in my lifetime.
Galaxies collide,
But not in my lifetime.

How shall I die then?
Blood takes long to drain.
I enjoy watching it leave.
I hear, "You have no idea
How confining being alive is."
The heart works and beats,
Runs, gallops, and you just stare ahead.
You never notice.
You are always in my mind.
There is no off switch,
No sanity switches to flick.
For years, you have wanted
The end for us,
The sleep, the nothing, the wonder.
If there is a God, he ignores us.
He enjoys knowing we know
Time is a hole in our duplicity.
He enjoys that I crave life.
That is the hook
I hang on.
We fail and fail many times
At the ritual of being.
Prisms reflect in shattered mirrors
While shattered mirrors

2014 Anthony C. Morgan

Photograph of American Model/Artist Chantel Bacon

Show prisms within prisms.
Temptation crashes into
The membrane of infinity.
Repetition since and forward.
Only skeptical impressions
Bounce to obscure my
Attempts, which crumble with my synapses' misfiring—
Always into solitude.
Remembering me, not you.
Poison chilling
Every crippling endeavor.
Glass piercing through us.
Scourged, swollen, and abstracted,
You outcast, you outsider—you, the entity
inside,
Diminished and tormented.
Ophelia and Desdemona
Crave tomorrow, crave sleep.
Talons deep and
Overwhelming.
A slight remembrance.
Thoughts in a storm cloud
Against a dreamy idealism.
While the diagnosis is being determined,
Reason disappears.

Photograph of French Model/Artist She nandoah

Tips of flames wink at infinity,
Leaving voices to explain,
With pain and anxiety, "I mend our purpose.
I am in here,
Incapable and unwanted."
Into nothing, into absence.
We: there is no such thing.
I, not you, am me.
Fool: I, not you, am I.
There are always echoes,
Echoes of self-defeat,

Echoes the vigilantes are tracking,
Echoes clinging from barbed-wire tears,
Never releasing.
I know there are no others.
I am all these voices in my head.
Corkscrewing into madness,
I dig my claws into
Your essence, with our first
Realization that our father
Knew he made a mistake.
Me the mistake.
The mistake has always been me.
My sister died.
Then you—you died.
But you made no exit.
You waited until my inception.
We, the singular duality.
Our exposition of mental relentlessness
Adhered to my intolerable psychosis.
You hide inside me.
Your soul and my soul: one blot of darkness.
You need to live.
I need to complete the witches' prophecy.
The demented act of a twin-thinking brain,
One has to exit.
Never scheduled to live,
I snuck under the birth realm, was
The drugged fetus
Who lived and who survives,
Precocious and brilliant.
My intellect examines itself.
Gauguin entered with colored visions.
He died and lived, vile with a tortured mind, one
Convoluted and demon-ridden like ours, like mine.
Beyond the planets, hate, obsessed and swelling, is
Beyond the angels, keeping score—

Beyond the nonexistent end.
The frugal forgiveness
Of nothing at all,
Of nothing at all.
My thoughts, your thoughts, our thoughts,
Of pain and punishment,
Of acid-rimmed eyes,
Of being whipped and bloodied
For all the sins since Christ died.
With that first slice, we knew it was right.
That evil and scum is our existence.
Oh, that perverted genius intellect
Never relenting, ever present,
Always being, producing a new paradox,
Always laughing,
Always hating, always despising
That which is within—every contemplation
Challenged with hatred,
A smile of lonely insecurity.
I have wanted to stab you,
Slice your throat,
Gut your genitals,
Behead you.
I have wanted to watch as we die.
I am sick of you, I am
Beyond the deaths that could have been
Dark moons,
Dark minds,
Dark rooms,
Dark abhorrence steeped in cowardice.
The snake coils like a female's love.
It dreams that life sustains beyond this awakening.
Impressions crash through the doors of perception.
Vile laments are what you scream inside us.
Merciless is the punishment
For the crimes against you.

*Photograph by Canadian photographer
Bonita (Bonnie) Harris*

Bleed,
Bleed,
Bleed.
Die, you unloved pretension.
Cozy up closer.
Catch a glint of the scalpel.
I will cut you.
You need to be in pain.
Then I will cut you again.
You need to be in more pain.
And I will cut you once more.
I love to feel the blade move across your face.
Think of simpler times, of lies you told
When you knew your likeness was lying.
Your life is a lie.
I cut you because I despise us.
Not in madness, but in retribution,
Till you/I/we are dead
With demons who will digest us.
Nothing,
Nothing,
Nothing prevails.
Not all minds go insane.
Some confess,
Some commit suicide.
Photoesque, abstract,
Metaphysical, and yet parasitic,
The saints collect their bets.
Placing us against a wall,
Philosophies our chosen mentality.
Ceres sucks hard on Calypso's breast,
Rainbows are created.
Nothing is what thinkers contemplate,
Yet
Something is the devourer of nothing.
Eyes are skewed with presumed expressions.

Another life steeped in vanity.
All sufficiently convinced.
I comprehend fantasy
Just death's indifference.
Hear them cheering.
Hear them discussing.
Hear them pretending they will not kill.
Deny the existence.
Succumb to the consequence.
Walk beside the tributaries.
Elastic inferences preclude disarmament.
I see the beginnings
Without images suffocating in delirium,
Without images refusing acceptance,
Without images abandoning reality.
Twisted outcomes
In time
Sanitize the belligerent sources,
The artist's genius
Sight unseen,
I look for comfort
Find daggers in my heart.
Blood, blood,
Blood, blood,
Blood defining life
In the chalices held up to water gods.
Stewing in remorse of lost attitudes,
Crimson in spectacular display,
My ashes spill into the ice caves, which
Vomit me over raging water.
Wet nuns in beds want
The pieces of me,
The remains of me,
The essence of me.
Indisposed to showing deference
Catapults vilifying my innocence, and

Alone with open wounds draining,
I survive to exemplify conflict.
Catching bullets,
Spooning over lost loves,
Drugged, unaccompanied, and unwilling, I see that in
All of the canvases I am painted upon,
My insistence is my own objection,
I am art defined by thought,
I am the Reformation.
I am desolation, born on consequences
Hierarchy trampling ghosts
Restraining hysterical laughter.
Tumbling through references of obscurity and
Knowing that fragility is effervescent,
I place the point of the knife.
I put pressure on the knife.
I watch blood begin to appear,
First quiet,
Then accusatory, and
Finally splendid.
Streams find a refuge in this sinner's bewilderment,
Decorating infatuation with distinction,
Sneering at the red-stained heavens.
My ideals misplaced under every woman,
Paralyzing, mischievous antecedents.
Synaptically psychopathic
Nightlife cannons explode
The pitfalls of inquisition.
There is light just above the guillotine.
There is sarcasm in shooting stars
I will lie extravagantly in order to possess knowledge.
You deliver full-mouth kisses with an eye to the camera.
The blade severs my head.
You appear in all those long-ago mysteries
Crotch less honeycombs ripped in an elevator.
Having scars because I have loved,

I am a contradictory prophet without a cross,
I search for myself among the illusions you present,
Stillborn as my brother I see you have shaved your center.
An arrow enters my neck.
I contemplate moving through time.
Guest composers take my drink order.
My vacuous words appear in your neon eyes.
Artists passing ask if my sperm is as sweet as my dreams.
Life ransacks all communication.
The windows are open; our sins fill every room.
From the fringe, I see you straddling Jesus,
Eliminating moving contrarily forward.
Land is sighted, so all the crew demands my curiosity.
I realize distance is only a concept if treaties can distinguish me from my ego.
Snakes collect. You squat as they glorify you
Unaccustomed to remorse, I watch my blood spill more and more.
Fatalities continue to follow.
Females always spring from my dilemma.
Awaking from the past, I view your opened vagina,
Amorphous and attracting shadows.
Trapped in my brain,
Thoughts glide beyond the apocalypse to a place
Where nothing can exist,
Not even the contours of irrationality.
Just a beneath.
Just a never completed deliberation.
Just gaseous neurons firing.
Flanked by vastness,
Carpenters' tools collide.
Sharpened edges penetrate.
My soul bleeds.
My brother draws the line,
A line from a lime's rind,
A line that instigates.
Yes, it is the line divine,
Known only in reflection and

Inexplicable to logic.

I take out my gun.
The soundtrack plays.
I smirk.
Drawing back the trigger,
I, Being myself
as me,
Shatter inconsolably,
Watching
Lady Macbeth nurse our child.

Artwork by Russian/Italian artist Tomaeva-Gabellini Fatima

QUOTING THE CYCLOPS

Disembarking.
Disassembling.
Disintegrating.

The worms reveal themselves.
Dripping blood into goblets,
Sailors sing myths and
Swill sarcasm
With streams of buoyed perversity.
Remembering the catastrophe, the
Holes in my hands, the
Scars in my imagination,
You masturbate in cafés.
I want to open your chest,
Climb in, and stitch us up,
Rush to see what you feel
When you stand unclothed before me,
A wayward catalyst
Melting away from corrosive tears,
Rewarded with the power of misfortune.
When in doubt,
We look at each other,
Pathetic marooned individuals
Pawing the earth for food.
Your breasts are inflated with chemicals;
My mind is filled with implants.
Living the worst existence,
We jump for the weapon.
You have sharp incisors
My thoughts slink away to Crystal Beach,
Sweet music from spaghetti westerns,
The sky turning smoky gray from water-soaked wood.

Your dagger across my neck, with you
Twisting it to show how deep love innervates us.
I reach for my mother's locket.
She rights all the wrongs.
Malaise retreats as the aftertaste remains.

The Germans march into France
While Chevalier sings "Notre-Dame De Paris" to Robespierre.
The Folies Bergère moves to Montreal.
Drunken sailors rehearse The Iliad in pubs.
All takes place on paper.
Yes, I am prepared for war.
Recalling the smell of your vagina,
I recreate influential dreams.
Priests dismiss your sins.
Your legs spread,
Jesus climbs the cross
Impressed by Picasso.
Nude ballet dancers play mime games.
We cling to each other in the basement,
Sex takes the place of our thoughts.
Poetry nourishes the illustrated falsehood.
Dali creates the word originality.
Afterward, we wipe our mouths
On each other, experiencing
Pleasure lingering.
We are solitary souls finding solace in
Signing our names with waves
That pound and spew,
Erasing all traces of us
Continually.
Yet we exist,
I think.
Anyway, that is what you said—
Or what I heard you say.

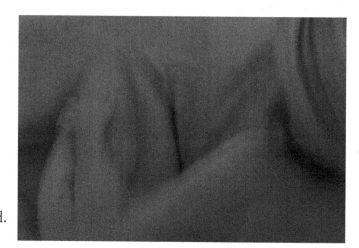

Photograph by Scottish photographer
Stuart McAllister

Without boundaries, Poseidon and Thoosa make love.
Scattered and still warm from reading Blake, I separate fear from fearlessness.
With the consent of Neptune, you kill all the men on board.
In the Mediterranean above Atlantis, I relearn why I am.
Baudelaire's spirit, guiding Whistler's, broadbands cross the horizon line.
The genius within us trolls the Evrotas, signaling for Edward de Vere to appear.
Emboldened by skeptics, we travel through an iris to reach rational comprehension.
Standing straight like a caryatid, you hold one naked breast while the other is tattooed.
When I lick your clitoris, venom replaces the milk of your soul.
Your immense beauty unfurrows with every thrust and spasm.
No illusion can replace the thirst created by adding more to plenty.
My biceps grows, my legs strengthen, and my eyes are those of a raven.
I am intellect in a cave, matched against my wit and enormous intellect.
Influenced by the movement of the seas, I cut, bite and rip into your breasts.

Stars need forgiveness because fools interpret only what they perceive.
You kiss me, and I am enamored with you once more.
The tears written in an image of cholera now huddle in menstrual desire.
Falling into your arrangement, I realize that your remark is stinging me.
Cold and calculating, you paint me outside the edges of this canvas.
Your whip opens my veins. The dimensions of pain expand into sensual recollections.
Licking wine from every lovemaking crevice, you crash upon me.
Your puckered legs, creased with relationship scars, rest heavily on me.
I hold you so I can disintegrate before my self-awareness tortures my delusions.
The beginning is the end; the dream is a nightmare; your shadow hovers.
Why is this opposite of being earth bound denying all my enigmas?
Laced to adversity, your body pulses, stiffens and spews what I have deposited.

"The Lark Ascending," "Golden Slumbers," and Miss Havisham:
Fairy tales told about misgivings before exile was fashionable.
Elixir harlequins at the steeplechase seek verification from non-existence.
You are the dominate silhouette on the moor making love to yourself as dogs howl.
I am aware when your lies whisper; they liberate the most disillusioned people.
That is why I chose to finger-paint filmstrips—so Heathcliff can endure endless pain.
I notice that artists who enjoy carte blanche celebrate sashay to the altar to lick you.
While men in capes infiltrate the mindless semen swimming upstream,

Wallowing in the warmth,
Wallowing in the flesh.
However, you and I remain in sorrow's reflection,
The brunt of Constance's hilarity lashed to the bow, treading water and believing in God.

Tortured by insignificance, I scream from the operating table.
Frozen inside without any doubt, the perfusion continues,
The chloroform eclipsing my blood, I am the wreckage I created.
Derelict amateur poets splash antidotes on my face.
My attitude remains undaunted;
You still fulfill my beliefs.
I cannot perform this drama without you.
Traveling quickly to caress you, I run out of my skin, my flesh and out of time.
For the God's to forgive me, I feel a harpoon push my heart through your destiny.
Cast on the angry waves, I hear you screaming for your last lover.
The honey haired daughter of a banished Saint you taught to obsess after every anal turnaround.
I hear my name, enabler of none—the ropes around me tighten.
That last lash split my eyes, yet my ambition is all I can see.
The anchor descends, securing that you be tethered to my destiny.
Water finds its way into me making love to my flesh as I make love to you.
Happier than I have ever been,
I want to say, "I miss you."
Sharks strike,
Red blood diluting what I have conceived
Brutus is the first to arrive.
I see myself in parts:
Long-ago pieces,
Long-ago memories,
Long-ago endeavors.
My resentment departs.
Eve's hand drops mine.
Storms swirl.
The abyss
Detaches from my consciousness,
Now entering

Aphrodite's womb.

There you are, my love,
Behind an eyelash,
Embracing another.

Yet again,
I am alone,
Alone,
With blood on my hands,
Alone
With blood on my hands.

Disembarked.
Disassembled.
Disintegrated.

Photograph by Canadian photographer Bonita (Bonnie) Harris

THE VOYAGE BEFORE TIME BEGAN TO CRY

Written with L. Thomson

The stench is in my mind.
The muskiness.

The claustrophobic walls.
The slime that is settling on me.

Yet Meursault is there.
He is just sitting there,

Slowly examining the streaming dust in the sunlight,
Slowly turning toward the distance in his mind.

I am not ready for life behind bars.
I am not that tragic figure.

Camus's most famous antihero.
Camus's imaginary existential thinker.

We are surrounded by the nemesis of thought.
We are the antecedents directed to surrender,

Mistaken for nothing at all,
Mistaken for resolutions inherent in the act of being.

Eyelids missed from the exotic spirit.
Eyelids never entering eternity.

In the morning, the cell is cold.
In my mind, Meursault smirks at me.

He understands that the winds of ignorance are bitter-tasting.
He understands we can never be the opposite of who we are.

I know he knows what emptiness is.
I cannot see my presence anywhere.

Guards pass. One hands me a straight razor.
Guards patrol in a circular loop, out of the ordinary.

Strict rules stripped of intelligence.
Strict measures on cultural suicide.

Laughter is variable, exhumed by natural disasters.
Laughter from the outside of the inside of fate.

Iconic murders on the loose for redemption.
Iconic saints in love with their admiration.

Bullets from boomerang recognition protest loudly,
Bullets form beautiful resistance heading nowhere.

Courtroom jesters tie me to the mast.
Courtroom stenographers beat me without mercy.

You in delicate lace, bending over for the jury to show your innocence.
You presenting your breasts as proof and pleading the case of my guilt.

Forgotten retaliation becomes the nemesis for further apprehension.
Forgotten amorous adventures in monotonous bedrooms.

Click!
Click!

I am in Patrick Hamilton's Hangover Square.
George Bone calls me over for a drink.
We are just old friends from the sanitarium where crazy people bleed frequently.

We both want to deconstruct those who cannot comprehend genius.

He tells me about how he loves Netta and wants to murder her.

Qualifying our absurd nuances, we exchange personalities.

However, all of this is just happening in my mind.

I am standing outside myself in search of searching for the search that will end my searching.

Bone and I visit Jack the Ripper, who suggests we should never become sane.

Maybe this time the starlight carousels will spin forward reintroducing how it started.

Colors on canvas formed from landscapes living inside Bone's mind diverts us once more.

You were nude, more than nude, pure nakedness, robust and warm yet undiscovered.

I confess I was proud to introduce you to the imaginary characters suffocating in my brain.

As mental wards cast doubt on my existence, you were spellbound to learn of my experiences.

While I am comforted in solitude, my singular thoughts began to assemble in parallel alignment.

Holding a gun, I became all the breeding distillations that culminate in Godly artistry.

Mischievous while I lay on the table, doctors line up their lobotomy instruments.

How is it scrutinizing of oneself leads to self-disappearance?

Click.

Click.

Interrogation.

Interrogation.

Is Leon a replicant? I am quickly inside Blade Runner.

Inconsistencies and hypocrisies are now the pit and pendulum that death rigs ride before me.

Am I Deckard or Batty? Human or a Nexus 6 model?

To survive, I must remember, "Eliminate all other factors. The one that remains must be the truth."

Survival in voyages and dreams means reversing the moment when allegations turn against belief.

It is easier to assume that omitting oneself from the thought of not having any thoughts leads to one's accommodation.

In plain sight, I can see the pedestal angels aiming their hypnotic illusions just ahead of me.

Unfolding in the space where Buddha once walked, I cleanse myself of past volatility

Priss knows that I am neither undercover nor eliminated – mirrors lie if abandoned.

Interrogation.
Interrogation.

Lorna, dressed for rapture, appears on screen.
Caught in the turnstile entering Harrods,
She spins
Beyond her escape, playing it aloof
Past the très chic museum where walls have bloodstains,
Where androgynous anorexics smoke Gauloises and
Wear outspoken clothing styles not yet fashionable,
Their eyes darkly smudged and concealing tormented souls.
Beatles songs are in cement and are indifferent to the footsteps upon them.
Ahead past Albert Hall, handsome Heathcliff,
With the allure of Lorelei, beckons Lorna.
Lorna, blue eyes wide, nipples poised, and panties moist, turns to her image.
She steals a ticket for the Fleet Street Tunnel,
Guaranteed passage to Hades Palace
A paranoiac theater for authors, artists, and debauchers.
Greedily, hungrily, she takes Heathcliff's arm.
Slim, leathered Elizabeth and Miss Wollstonecraft leave the nightclub where comic duo Edgar
and Linton headline.
They enter a Turkish bath where their objections produce voluntary hallucinations.
Heathcliff strikes a match, enlightening egos and condemning love moral insanity.
In a tiny hotel room in Vienna, Freud undresses Lorna, pointing out how easily buttocks welt
from a whipping.
Casanova bursts through a stained-glass window, rescuing Lorna.
She is in the queen's naked lap; the two kiss and retire to the opposite of certainty.
This complex plot, its author with dreams of insistence, harmonizes with ships set to sail.
Lorna, with destructively sexual interventions, begs Heathcliff to handle her.
Suffering from ombrophobia, I sneak under dresses, probing for infallibility.
You catch me on film: an incendiary maniac with cadaver-like spasms.
I kneel before Lorna. She squats, knowing that my presence assures impossibilities.
Elizabeth, rising though night and fog realizing her suicidal ideations displays hysteria.
Inside an ocular rainbow, Gudrun Brangwen pensively defends indifference.
As the clubfooted Philip still craves love, his reflection shatters his mirror.
Basil Hallward completes his masterpiece about suspiciousness and hedonism.

All the cracked windows in the Tower of London reveal a torment that will never end.
Heathcliff travels on the moors past the hound to a grotto where beatific Cathy glows.
Fellini hates this script, this scene, and this movie.
Anna Magnani simply stares at the camera.
Fade out.
Cut to snow falling heavily.
Lorna, now playing the Wife of Bath, smiles coyly. She slowly undresses while walking toward us, walking toward us until she is pure, naked loveliness evolving beyond all narratives.

Fin. The credits roll as the Endeavour arrives in Cooktown.

Click,
Click.

I fall back to sleep. Am I now in the reality I have dreamt of encountering?

Click,
Click.

The night is very deep and black, a sensual backdrop encoded against renegade admissions.
A bedraggled man is shoved into the cell; he has been beaten badly and is covered with blood.
Meursault steadies the man, placing him on the bed, then begins to wipe his face.
The man snaps his fingers for me to bring him a cup of water.
His hands have holes in them, and his forehead is punctured and bleeding.
I hand him a cigarette, he smiles.
Meursault asks him if he is the one who began time.
Thought awakens. What was up is down, and what was thought is REM sleep.
The three of us are in a café in Pigalle, looking impeccable in black Italian silk suits.
Jesus runs his hand through his long, black hair and places his ivory-handled cane on the table.
The Busby Berkeley number begins. A hundred, naked women jazzing to "Moonlight Serenade."
Frank Sinatra unbuttons his bell-bottom sailor pants while Ava turns to Hemmingway.
Cole Porter in the lounge speaks with Fitzgerald about uncertain semantics.
I search the faces for a Swede, but my eyes darken, seeing juxtaposition in modern art.
Then, without warning, the war begins. I look for my father to protect me.
The bombs are calico orange with streams of reflective fabrication—apathetic to philosophical heights.

Paris is settled again with bemused artists in love with the facets of themselves that disintegrate.
Kerouac commits symbolic suicide because the waiter remembers only Coleridge.
Uneasy about their bullet wounds, the judges view women as abject evil and corrupt.
I collect sheets from the hotel, tie the ends of misfortune, and mail them to illusionists.
As all the horses dash to the finish line, I explore examples of renegade retaliation.
Metaphysical Italians plot the movement of planets while making love to Canadian explorers.

Almost a full click.
Almost a full click.

Disney characters reverse roles, playing reality. And I, I am now just a sketch on white paper, waiting to be completed. You, you! Can you read me?

Completed click.
Completed click.

I rape women, kill unarmed soldiers, and confiscate property while wearing a crucifix.
Yes, I am the substitute saint sharing the sins made infamous by Madame Bovary.
In a meeting with futurists, I am told I exist only in my mind.
I run from this realm and notice I have outdistanced my body.
Thoughts I have linger, though memories switch sides.
When the sun peaks into the asylum, I sit up with a large shard of glass in my arm.
The drugs warm my view. The nurse asks me about the old days, about Woodstock.
My refection is idealistically sepia and outdated.
Young accountants ask me to follow quietly.
Their misfortune is my life is the one they will never live.
My thoughts tie knots to what comprehended and sell them to jewel thieves.
Simplifying things, Meursault hands me an eraser.
In exchange for a realistic assessment, Michelangelo spreads God's legs.
Young lovers, hand in hand, find themselves sauntering along the Danube.
He kisses her as she kisses her as she kisses him kissing him.
The blur continues as I cry about each tear I produce.
The lieutenant tosses me the screenplay for A Night at the Opera.
Outside in the strange world, they ask if my inabilities are my defense.
I sit in a chair facing twelve women who are smoking hashish and fondling each other.
Meursault says I had a fair trial because all thought at any moment is subjective.

I am guilty of living and freely thinking, though this is all in my mind.

Vultures arrive on gravestones as prostitutes die continually from deceptive truths.

All the beautiful blue merle collies, the mild-tempered shih-tzus, and the happy dachshunds in those unread chapters search the distance for more to sniff.

Click.
Click.

Nevertheless, it is too late.
It is too late, Meursault states.
Too late.
Too late.
All must return to their stories.

Photograph by Scottish photographer Stuart McAllister

THE TWINNING OF BOADICEA

Written with L. Thomson

I recognized you
Before we met.
I knew you
Before I spoke.

From off stage, I peeked at you.
You knew I was there.
You basked in the applause.
Your performance: brilliant again.
You could not see me,
Entombed in contemplation,
Blinded by the lights.
A performance of seduction.
I, too, am seduced.
Circe was right.

Your intellect and vanity:
Unwavering servants to your ego.
All those sad virtues of the sainted are
Disguised as obedience.
I envy you charming them.
You are natural.
Passion pervades
On the other side of the moat.
Sealed within, without us all,
Your enigma remains.

I loved you before the war.
Resonating in an unfamiliar place, you
Your gait, your cadence,
Your self-assured strut,

Photograph by German photographer Susanne Kreuschmer -- www.susanne-kreuschmer.de, make –up Katrine Jakobsen – model Patrizia Balcer (Facebook Patrizia Fotomodel)

Your smile, your voice—all
Bore admission,
Reaching deeply
Through the trellis,
Fashioning a visceral tether and
Gently consuming me.

Boadicea seeks Minerva's counsel.
While Electra yearns for revenge,
Aeolus quietly muses
Keats ponders the physical.
On deck, Gilmore plots his course.
Calypso is the last to reach Messalina.
Narcissus nods to Hester Prynne.
Your soft lips find me.
We blend on a confident wave,
Entering Athena's warm womb.

Wisdom arrives on horseback,
Delivered by a menstrual Godiva.
Tempted, I decline the invitation,
Preferring instead Pandora.
Divine encounters.
My breasts need rewarding.
Find inside me our eternity,
A fury of cascading echoes.
I am a star, a compass,
Anticipating penance.

I wait for the theater to empty.
Still, the mystery resonates.
A wake of candles and liquor.
We are all faithless lovers,
Whores who entice.
You see another
Undressing her. Having me.

Observations reveal themselves.
Klimt paints me in gold.
Penelope knows my thoughts.

Clichés and trite expressions
Crawl from my mind to my mouth,
Seeking to fashion, to find, to know
This canvas stretched across me,
Brilliant and attentive.
My reverie is inflamed.
Nakedness overcomes beauty.
You have forgotten, forgotten.
My apparition is your shadow
Trapped in a past reality.

I recognized you
Before we met.
I knew you
Before I spoke.

*Photograph by German photographer Jens
Neubauer – model Sabrina Beyer*

DREADFUL QUESTION-BLOODY ANSWER

I bludgeon
You,
Then forgive myself
For another
Encounter
With raging language.
Against modern scrutiny, I
Crash down
Pillars with Circe
While you
Slip
Oxytocin fishhooks
Into my thoughts
I am here,
Alone on the ocean,
Experiencing the numbness
Of hypocrisy.
The dead die once more.
Split heads and fragments.
The arbitrary prison
Condemning us to
Austerity.
Mutiny of conscience
Erupting.
I confront myself,
Handing you the implement
Of my death.
Stabbing, stabbing
Incomprehension magnified.
Remembering the Sphinx.
The gods making love,
Causing the equinox.

Photograph by German photographer Jens Neubauer – model Sabrina Beyer

I descending
Into masked, lost, and decaying
Poetry.

Athena sends me a dagger.
You and I dig
For pretense inside my chest.
Dysfunctional apparitions.
Messages to Zeus.
Obsessive opposition.
On the seventh day
As he rested,
Not knowing the outcome,
"Nevermore" entered his mind.
Zero would be the beginning.
No longer innocent,
Ravaged by slashing waves, and
Unapologetic, I stand
Over your bleeding body,
Covered in questions of why,
Discounting my gestures
But not my motives.
Insane yet
Able to implode.
The whale follows the ship.
Scorpions mate.
On the fringe of thought,
The reservoirs
Of rumors form
Tributaries,
One moving in the direction of absurdity;
The other, the theater.
Miró on my mind.
Munch in my mind.

Minimalist breasts as art.
You instigate
Lustful revenge,
A pitiful torture.
My knees buckle.
Your laughter is testimony,
Louder than insight.
Always the disapproval.
Using punishment
For circumstantial evidence.
Then the numerous
Me's, I's, and imposters
Reach beyond myself.
Reality is too constraining.
Eventually, thought
Asks about how and why.

On the tribute platform,
Arrows pierce my heart.
Blood, my favorite manuscript,
Accounts for
Men and lost brothers
Stolen by the sea.
Penance.
Cruel and unrelenting,
I leave the fantasy,
Waiting for those
Willing to be nailed,
While Menelaus
And Telemachus
Watch Francis Drake agonize
About the foreground.
Chastised by medieval
Inquisitors,
Several sons fall from grace.
Tortured by your return,

I accept the scars that
Wrack my inner soul
And disapprove of
My existence
As a sinner.

Who will die?
In search of repentance
And philosophy,
You enabled me
To suck persistently
At your nipples.
I feel accustomed,
Both in need and within,
To rewarding you.
But
The sails are torn.
Land is an illusion.
I will never return.
On board to hell,
Painters sacrificed.
Scapegoats are found
Among the tenderhearted.
The whip
Comes down on
Billy Budd's back
And
Comes down
On your back
And
Comes down
On my back.
You never cover your eyes.
It is all
Deceptive imagination.
I exist to kill

Us both,
Yet the nuance
Escapes the purpose.
Your gentleness
Closes the gap
Of absurdity.
Bloodstained and
Lacking influence,
Except for death,
You can hear it.
If you last,
If you are last,
Your brain ignites
What I have forever
Never felt.

There was a moment
Of enlightenment
With Dylan Thomas
In the asylum
Listening to cutters
Whose
Insanity was insured
As light and doom
Searched infinity.
Your skirt drops.
Your panties follow.
Next, your legs
Raise and spread.
The question repeats itself:
"Have you killed before?"
Oedipus
Rides on a sacrifice
From a strong wind,
Like lava spewing.

Photograph by Scottish photographer Stuart McAllister – model Sarah Mua

More destruction:
The walls need to come down.
Conquer Troy.
Conquer mortals.
Conquer and kill.
Charge with a trumpet.
Cannons in tow.
Fire arrows and spill molten liquid from cauldrons.
Trample the flowers
Above my grave.
Illusions vanish.
I compare my genius
To that of those who create works of veneration.
Scissors cut.
Matchsticks burn.
Words define me.
You define me.

In their final withdrawal,
Seasons are indifferent
To the uncontested
Menacing of the
Wounded gods
Who cancel destiny.
I feel only pain.
The label on my mind is
Branded to combat waves that are
Too high to be sincere.
Broken vows.
Angels arrive
On the shore,
Disheveled and bewildered.
They wave.
Ignoring me
They lick your womb.

Sounds prevail.
Music nourishes intelligence.
Soft choral voices offer incentives.
I ask for alternatives.
Splendor dissolves.
Nothing is denied.
Those appearing to be far
Are below my eyes,
Sleepwalking from their lives.
Extremities bear no grudges.
Bodies bob.
Lightning attends to us.
God assigns me the task.
I approach the underworld,
Cleaver and alert,
Absent yet aware.
I leave as I live
After an upheaval.

You are bedding more.
A child and yet another.
These days:
The monotony of comfort.
Breasts always being
Handled;
Games, played.
The chariot races.
Finding your mark.
The miraculous scent
Between your legs
Wafting,
Encouraging earthquakes,
Coalescing stampedes and disasters.
In glorious persuasion,
A noble hero's
Dress rehearsal is an

Allegory for the universe.
Gods watch
For humans to awaken.

Those aging faces.
I taunt the evil
That arose,
Cursing that bit
Digging at my mouth.
There is nothing,
Nothing but decay.
Being lost is our salvation.
Crying in agony,
Cicero writes letters.
A dove lands on my shoulder.
Just as the axe strikes
Us both,
He is eaten. I am charged
With murder.
Caravaggio, my attorney,
Surprises the jury.
David has the head of Goliath.
I am guilty.
I am a poet.
My identity is temptation
To this world
Of accomplished necessities.
Hypocrisy.

It is you,
You the mistress,
Naked on the stern,
Exposing your buttock,
Showing a soul of thorny roses.
You watch me
In silhouette.

My hands tighten.
Deprived of benefit,
I can only transport
Myself to a canvas,
To a poem,
To a sentence,
To a mere instant.
Our tragedy,
Apart from the roar,
Is now
Simply a forgotten
Desire.

I am to be drawn and quartered
For using my imagination
To startle their thoughts.
Measuring the frontier,
Ulysses champions truth
Moreover, kills the aggressors.
Virgil writes about the escape.
Calypso warns me that
Second choices beget nothing.
I steal the black stallion
And ride.
Days pass.
Weeks turn to months;
Months, to years.
The gods
Made me swear
To kill without feeling.
I killed,
Then I killed more.
And the absurdity
Of believing
In death
Diminished into a comatose

Photograph of American Model/Artist Chantel Bacon

Obsession
When my arms were bloodied and scarred.
Hermes arranged a meeting with Athena.
She told me,
"Music never leaves the mind.
Think in scales.
Get inside the melodies."
Between the sarcastic
And the profound,
Poseidon arranged
For me to meet Scylla
Where
Virgins reign.
Sex is the price to pay.
The sweet songs of those passing
Rustle the sheets on the unmade beds.
I know you have been here.
I can smell you.
Making love passionately,
I feel your mouth,
Not hers. I feel
Your legs welcoming me.
Coleridge praises us.

Coltrane
Makes the unenlightened
Think and
Then think again,
Think once more.
Then thinking becomes thought.
Thought becomes awareness.
Awareness baffles
Those hanging from a rope.
My friend Don Giovanni
Arrives,
Never settling

For the illusions I have arranged for him.
He adapts
Rolling train refrains
To his
Changing dreams and temperament
While
Comparing the truth and cadence
Of
Random women calculating communion.
Circe makes me love her.
I cannot tell time.
Sunrises and sunsets depend on my mood.
Intoxicated. In pencil and on paper,
Words, like a banner,
Solicit my attention.
Finally, they come for me.
Another war.
Another prologue.
In chains and drugged, I experience
Delirium.
Final check:
Catastrophic.
Madness.
Insanity.
Yet thoughts remind me
Of before the before.
I am remembering
Me, an epic sailor
Sailing toward illogical providence and
Questioning ethics.

You were there in my bed,
You as her—her as you.
Her, the her I have been fantasizing about.
Her—the her—beauty unrenowned.
Penelope in all their eyes.

I am not Ulysses.
I am words—pushing barriers
Farther than constellations.
My love is pure.
The detours of my search
Are completed.
I am home.
We make love and celebrate.
The wine is
Darker than blood.
I am again me.
Your brown eyes
Widen.
You
Bludgeon me,
Then, hand in hand
With God,
You simply
Forgive yourself.

Photograph of French Model/Artist She nandoah

SHE WILL ARRIVE UNDER STORMY SKIES

The right encounter
Will lead one to scorn any expression
Of death.

The right punishment
Will lead one to scorn any challenge
Of sympathy.

The right answer
Will lead one to scorn any disappointment
Of one's willingness.

The right fascination
Will lead one to scorn any reality
Of insistence.

The right experience
Will lead one to scorn any disbelief
In necessity.

The right attitude
Will lead one to scorn any admiration
Of faith.

The right conditions
Will lead one to scorn any possibility
Of weakness.

The right difference
Will lead one to scorn any construct
Of community.

Photograph by Scottish photographer
Stuart McAllister

The right image
Will lead one to scorn any admission
Of complicity.

The right contact
Will lead one to scorn any warning
Of separation.

The right threat
Will lead one to scorn any curse
Of eternity.

Shadows on webs.
The spider knows that
Life darkens.
Living in shallow,
Conscious ignorance and
Resorting to murder,
The crowned slaves
Butcher the aristocrats,
Leaving thought
To the reckless,
With hanging
On their minds.
Different spectrums
Rip insight.
I remember
A poet who said,
"All men shall be sailors."
But all sailors
Believe that
Christ walked
Past them.

Scorn eternity.
Scorn separation.

Scorn complicity.
Scorn community.
Scorn weakness.
Scorn faith.
Scorn necessity.
Scorn insistence.
Scorn willingness.
Scorn sympathy.
Scorn scorning.

I am the living
Testament to
Tortured insomnia,
The insects fidgeting
Inside my brain.
Ordered personalities are
A train station
For tarnished,
Opposing degrees,
Of life on the edge.
Pulsing, traversing,
And expressing
Suspicious differences.
Imitation admiration.
Corners becoming corridors.
Past mystery and
Beyond realization
To solitude,
Quenched by
Phantoms.
Weary of pure reason.

Confrontation.
Disappointment.
Reality.
Disbelief.

Photograph by Scottish photographer Stuart McAllister

Admiration.
Possibility.
Construction.
Admission.
Warning.
Curse.

The correct demise
Despises sanctuaries.
Steeped in momentous
Frivolity,
Death roars
In laughter.
Every notion is a scene,
Never a corollary.
Clusters of mothers' breasts,
Thighs and fluid flesh.
God is illusory,
Lily-colored silk.
Lavender fields and
Warmth:
All one collage
Trespassing space.
Everything private,
Uninterrupted nakedness,
Splendor.
Al di là di amore ammissibile
Permanente senza uscite.

Mordred in black
Enters. His
Eyes widen.
The round table
Collapses
Without conscience.
An alternative ending is

Permissible.
Techniques
Bedded in nightmares
Displace each other,
Brother for cousin,
Son for father.
An ingenious imposition.
I am beside Calypso,
Thrusting at a joust,
Fingers up,
Fingers down.
We all read the news today
about a lucky man who'd made
the grade.
Undulations between the ages.
Consciousness threatened.
Flip my sovereign
Octavius or Caligula to create
Geometric counterbalances.
Beethoven conducts without
hearing.
Ballet dancers love innovation.
Writers drink.
Poets strip for attention.
Soldiers march.
Treachery breeds.

Artwork by Italian artist Angelo Graziano – model Logan Zonas

I have six bullets,
Just six.
I have a bowie knife,
Just one.
I have hope,
God on the cross,
Flesh on the cross,
His hands with bloody holes in them.
The children rock in their cradles.

Jesus leaves Mary sleeping.
While he rolls away a rock, he says to me,
"That which was before can reverse from the center before time remembers being."
The world sings, loves, and dies
As a concert
In actuality.
The world is a bomb
Within an opera,
Within thought, and
Without presence.
Atomic.
Nuclear.
Common Core.
Ebonics.
Stupidity.
Greed.
After a drink,
Jefferson hands me my pistol.
An aircraft carrier
Appears.
I tell the crew
We shadow war.

Punishment.
Answer.
Fascination.
Platitudes.
Attitude.
Conditions.
Difference.
Image.
Contact.
Threat.

Needles.
Long knitting needles

Ram into ears.
Eyes are removed with cut glass.
Lips ripped.
Nose burned.
A straight razor
Straps leather,
Telling time.
Hands grip bricks.
There is no
"Sanctuary."
The arrows,
The spears, fly.
Balzac, Lelut, and T. S. Eliot
Use umbrellas
To deflect missiles
Between lifetimes
In hell.
Mental capacity
Is simplified,
Very simplified.
Watching humans
Killing humans.
Humankind is God.
God is humankind.
Humanity is flawed.
Therefore, God is flawed.
If repetition is
Learning, then
Murder must
Be a divine
Action.

Madness is the death of reality.
Reality is the death of madness.
Madness or reality—
Which is your weapon?

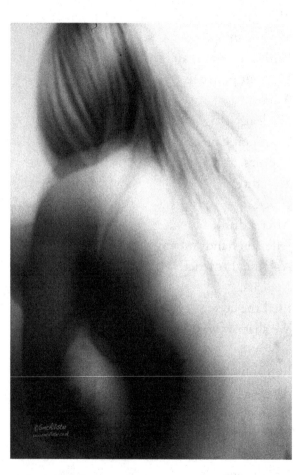

Photograph by Scottish photographer Stuart McAllister

A Surreal Entrance and a Suicidal Exit

Hatred,
The tie that vines
Expectation.
Just
Indirect heroism.
Wishing on stars
Colliding.
In thoughts,
Forever stirred
By reawakening.
All that is
Tempting is
Stitched
According to
Poetic tales,
Singling out the lonely
Forlorn outcasts
Who are voyaging
For redemption.

Victor and Elizabeth

Reason,
The tie that misinterprets.
Pitting
Tranquility
Against pleasure,
Using the
Final analysis
Instinctively
To denounce

Those poised
Inside a reflection
Of self-adoration.
Prolific criticisms
Invoke
Aggrandizement.
Desiring another's
Fortune.
Disappearing from
Heart into mind.

Des Grieux and Manon

Temptation,
The tie that defines.
Idiosyncratic
Manifestations
Confronting passageways
Set afire
By cravings.
Beyond duplicity is
Undiminished certainty.
That felicity
Strengthens one's internal
Need
To satisfy
Unquenchable
Tidings,
To fulfill
Villainous adventures
Unremorsefully and
Without consequence.

Lord Macbeth and Lady Macbeth

Regret,
The tie that untangles
The mind
From concepts.
Forming within
Acknowledgement,
The locket
Of the forlorn
Melts belief,
Mixing it with indifference
And fruity wine.
The lost heroine
Is in bed with artists
Confirmed as mad,
Resigned to the opposite
Of forgiveness.
Wanting the whips
Across their backs,
Bloodied and continuous.

Philip and Mildred

Repulsion,
Of the avenged
The tie that tangles.
Hardened encounters
On ladders,
Tying knots
So that bodies swing.
Faith, not genius,
Seeks amnesty
For one who sold virtues.
A phenomenon on its way
To restitution.
Death-rattle merchants
Apprise Mary

At the infirmary. They are
Idealists with daggers
From another realm. They
Kill the under thoughts
With their spectral contention.

Harry and Hermione

Trust,
The tie that weakens.
The mental disorder
Squirms
And imagines
That which is excessive
Demolishing
The framework
Of coincidence,
Replacing what was
With today.
Cavalcades nourish
Impressions,
Resolve issues
With untold
Expectations.
Swords are drawn;
Statements, made;
Bodies, buried.

Hedda and Eilert

Sorrow,
The tie that lingers.
Internally,
Death clings
To wonder,
A fraudulent

Correspondence
Dismissing
Sleep garbed
In dissonance.
Trails and excessive
Indignation
Streaming.
Hopeless
Thorns wrapped in tears,
Digging furrows,
Scorning memory
With an
Oblique shadow.

Heathcliff and Catherine

Silence,
The tie that probes.
Those who
Run despondently
Into crumbling walls
Dream of a disposed
Romanticism, a
Painfully
Enamored demoralization,
Clawing at throats,
Bleeding
From illusions,
Confounded by
Anthologies spread
With Golden Age
Simplicity, with
Purist enlightenment.
Eyelids close:
Damnation eternal.

Tristan and Isolde

Murder,
The tie that perplexes,
One requiring
Absence
Of memory,
Not spiritualistic
Reverence
For the seething pain
From an unsatisfactory
Experience.
Descent
Confounded by presumption.
The mind churns
Disbelief
Into induced
Misfortune,
Rattling the consequence
With nature's
Merciless undertow.

Oedipus and Jocasta

Cynicism,
The tie that differentiates
Amusing
Overtures from
Camouflaged
Transcendence.
Self-impressed
Intelligence
Milked over.
Subjects disregarded.
Adhering to
Presumed

Annihilation
Not previously
Investigated
By pillory expletives
Unknown
To resolved intelligence and
Innocent of reflection.

Gatsby and Daisy

Happiness,
The tie that antagonizes.
That links all things
Corroded
With maleficent
Hypocrisy,
Letting the mind
Foully develop
From meaningless,
Nondescript
Inner turmoil.
Lost in lush
Resentment
And gradual decay.
Crude fulfillment
Giving injury
To blatant
Laughter
Distilling in the brain.

Pelléas and Mélisande

Love,
The tie that betrays.
Unbounded
In its lust
For regret.

Selfish and finished,
Crowned
With thorns that
Pierce through
Time.
Nothing exempted.
Poisoned
Hooks;
Venom spreading.
Anguish
Without regard
Deteriorating
Reality's hold
Defiantly.

Paris and Helen

The brokenhearted
Remain unfearful.
We lumber together,
With no land in sight.
Though we have escaped,
Our fulfilment is futile.
Awkward in chains.
Convoluted by dreams.
Demeaned.
Waiting for
Corrections.
Earthly no more.
Dwindling
Because of our hopelessness.
I see your face
Writing poems
And coloring canvases.
It is all I embrace
As the ship sinks.

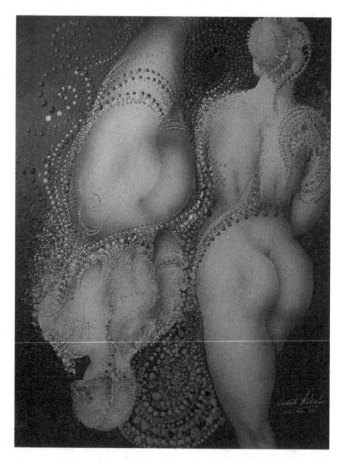

Artwork by Spanish artist Modesto Roldan

COURTESY OF WAR ALLEGATIONS

Saxophones from the fifties reclaim attention.
The seas roar in reminisced madness.
Privileged warriors are introduced on the Hellenistic stage.
Revolutionary jazz spreads worldwide.
Ulysses in San Francisco listens to Armstrong.
The captives are unforgiving after the bombing attempts.
I am a "cool" artist in Newport,
Stabbing my wrists with forked stilettos.
The blood leaves me to embrace you.
Statues in Ithaca cry for Rome.
Political conspiracies are heard by sailors.
Paratroopers are dying without remorse.
Soma institutions are recreating hysteria.
Insanity is dwelling in the marshlands of absurdity.
Literary choirs are sentenced for their belligerence.
Divorced wanderers are crazed with renown.
Carnivorous rumors infect Greek philosophers.
Goldman and I are having lunch with Ralph and Piggy.
Battlefield casualties are condoned by Lincoln.
You sit on the sofa with solid gold dildos,
Mailing invitations for quartets of suitors.
Aphrodite reaches for the forbidden apple.
Goddesses sing "The Gloria" for Euripides.
I meet you behind backboards for oral sex.
Diana, with huge breasts and thin hips, has
A leather catch for her arrows and sentiment.
She is playing cards with Cassandra, who cheats and makes allegations.
Envious with miscalculations of love
And missing the Mediterranean target,
The Greeks ultimately prevail.
Iphigenia surfs for Renaissance Italians.
Redefining a composition for cyclic epics,

I lick your lips and satisfy my appetite for inevitability.
I have clandestine meetings with Telephus in Ithaca.
We go nightclubbing. We sell Oracle nominations.
With his dementia, I hear Joyce redesigning language.
The atmosphere is one of bewilderment and gunpowder-induced amnesia.
Tapestry cartoonists sprinkle torment onto the arbiters of love.
Stinging creations toy with unsuspecting meanderers.
Diaphanous sails flutter in disregard.
Imperative battles linger in a solitary commentary.
Distinguishing rapture from agony's suicide,
Faust and his Devil have gambling fever.
Beauty is just beyond their comprehension,
Painted transparent with fairy-tale illusions.
Nocturnal expurgations are like gilded twilight.
Endless contemplation I engage in, noting a wave's mannerism,
Obsessing about every concubine's adventurers.
Anal quartermasters hunt for enemies to rape.
Character misfits are on loan for purposes of mistaken identity.
I see rowers with arrows embedded in their necks.
We are the creatures of necessity,
Anticipating watermark battles and naked rewards,
Reconciliation agreements with gods in love, their contrary
Splashing, bathing, and submerging of
Revolutionary enemies killed on sight.
Innocent blood shares synonyms, ignoring equilibrium,
Whether in thought or in memory.
I am rewriting inconsistencies to make parodies of perfection.
Outer shapes; inner images.
Land sighted in a golden brilliance.
I am chatting with Tzara in the galley.
Radical characteristics overshadow death's rumblings.
Surgeons on call treat maniacs from paranoiac vulgarity.
Crashing from a terminal idea, reality swims in Neptune's realm.
Accidentally landing in Mysia, Achilles moves on to Scyros.
Telephus, now a derivative, finds his finger in Deidamia.
All lines cross the future dead who have numbers on their backs.

Picasso asks to referee a grudge match between Munch and Leonor Fini.

Inflicted with wounds of distraction, I see you bathing with nymphs.

Cardiac allies share a Mediterranean disrespect for exploding cathedrals.

Sophocles, in splendor, thinks about raping Sophia on screen.

Courtship antipasti are served on the body of Hippolyte.

Penthesilea and the Amazons see the beauty of Paris against the gall of Achilles.

When the Vikings arrive, they commence to draw sketches of sadistic women.

The increasing boredom makes singular killing events more necessary.

Celts listen to the American Revolution and Hồ Chí Minh on BBC Radio.

Civilization has reached a shattering conclusion, warring for a woman's flesh.

Championed as a defector and an incurable romantic, Hitler plays chess with himself.

Occasioned by partisan simplicity, merchants sell human souls in religious relics.

Mermaids on the loose resolve issues from lower levels by denying sexual favors.

Having witnessed the sideshow of dismemberment, the Greeks accept heroism.

Ungrateful that the world is at war, people of émigré communities prepare to protest.

Once I speak with Mahler, he and I decide to share our shattered disappointments.

The absurd blacks sell each other quickly before being sold themselves.

Stormy seas with blood and dead bodies find seagulls and vultures feasting.

Trojan women are passed around by soldiers, like snakes used at prayer meetings.

There are fishing nets with catches of uniforms and fleshless resurrection armor.

Whores from Sicilian and Sardinian temples trawl for small but quick opiates.

Eros stops at the door, offering Hermes a night of pleasure.

When he is bent over for show, the obvious themes trump the false narratives.

Oracles, weaving hemp from barbarian encounters, slit their wrists for actors.

Funeral-pyre magicians' watch as Achilles kills the son of Poseidon.

Parallel inquiries from malcontents in unharmonious rapture form the aftermath.

Waves roll over bodies on the shoreline as conquest fountains spew blood.

What is the essence of knowledge and freedom?

The face that launched a thousand ships.

Like tectonic plates, epochs grate over one another.

Never stopping, Guinevere asks Arthur, "What do the simple folk do?"

Ships pass:
Heavenly dreams.
Nights end.
Desires implore

Neverlands and future escapades.
Dynamic archeological turns do not languish.
Clusters of literary genius face "The Waste Land" and "In Flanders Fields."
Amorous investigations border toxic understandings.
Questions annihilate any intelligent answers.
Tri-ribbon stripes appear on corporate national flags.
I am preoccupied with insinuation.
The laurels unravel and become spiked testaments.
Uncertain footsteps anticipate quarrelsome encounters.
Bursting forward, the madmen unsheathe and swing their swords.
Swinging,
Maiming,
Killing.
Certain that creation consisted of only one episode.
His ankles on fire, Mercury escapes the carnage.
I find myself again across a divide. Love is inaccessible to me.
The sound from the keyboard laments for May's anticipation and
Receive December's accusations of resolve.
Hospital corridors weep with limps.
Graphic icons are naked for inspection.
Chloroform: the ability to save fables without confliction.
Quenched hangman egotists wait for alcoholic reinforcements.
Beneath it all, I hear the call for young lovers to separate.
I forget which war this is and if I am dead or just waiting.
Quiet time.
Glenn Miller.
Affairs to remember.
Moments to cherish.

Down the hall, I see serenity as irresponsibility.
I take out my dagger and carve your name in my ego.
The London police in the dank tunnel ask about waters deep and uncrossed.
I love my blood, a blessed confirmation reminding me I am alive.
On the hills, I run to catch the dark clouds, your letters of introduction to death.
Who can uncover the madness of artists who are more wrathful than expected?
Aristotelian sympathizers roll me on my back as fire engulfs the room.

After discussing issues about the Rhineland, I engage with stars, ignoring mortals.

Tacks in my eyes and pins in my ears. Blood is secondary to the sound of your heart.

Free from domicile infringement, a murderer's persona appears, not my shadow.

The strings outplay the horns, leading me to the outskirts of what it is I am seeking.

Cocaine and crystal meth begin to whisper, deceiving those who are ultra-artistic.

Spread the genius and spare the minimalist. Never stop the ringing of iron bells.

Fingers on triggers, hands on handles: life is one more Cole Porter melody.

Obnoxious prison air outmaneuvers the jacks dealt to ancient gay philosophers.

A pallid alabaster hero encounters the slick trances of misinterpreted immortality.

Heaven's angels are fighting for access to Gethsemani Abbey

Hell's innocent, crying.

I concentrate on my own warm blood flowing,

That warm flow

Down my chest, thighs, and legs, and onto the white marble floor.

I have the hypnotic knowledge that I am me running from myself.

My invincibility outmaneuvered, I recognize the mirror's image wearing my skin.

Libertine speculators separate the divine, earthy women from the lecherous whores of society.

I am to die like Prometheus, always and forever,

For committing the crime of wanting more when seeing myself with less.

Mirrors, both shattering and apostolic, reflect how nothing emerges.

With my heart held out as penance, the incompetents' laughter roars.

Tranquil child after child is shoved into the ovens – it was, is, and will be.

Tears run down an elephant's face. The elephant then comes to my rescue.

She asks, "Why." She asks, "Why."

I have no answer.

A tribesman sticks an arrow in the elephant's eye and traces history home to Neverland.

Living with my appearance, I realize that I know there is no righteousness,

Just the relief of knowing that nothing is qualified for demand.

Where is the basement in which Plath hid?

I need it now, fifty years later.

This world hates its own inhabitants,

Despising all who cannot produce what the powers need.

The upheaval of arresting the ignorant who have only asked questions.

Zero tolerance—global markets—artists hung for creating.

The world loves God, knowing that simplicity is a vanilla attempt at gaining immortality.

Aristocrats swear to kill Poe's raven when Adam Smith arrives.

Slaughtering for fortune and ambition,

I am wanted for exiting a womb, for living and not existing.

Tarot cards hang from heavily scented violets and muffle danger.

Having an end to hatred and war is always just the always,

Always and before,

Before and always,

And always

And always.

According to Blake, hell is the next intersection.

Life is a corollary full of absence and advanced limitations.

Endless delusions are authentic when beheld as the mind decays.

Poetry is the format of the crazed reaching out to the bewildered for sympathy.

Lonely in themselves, the dismissive girls love me in idyllic infatuation.

Then there in the rye of Caulfield, you and I stare out and misunderstand,

Both of us thinking of the consequences of human deception.

Time has gone in the direction of recurrent Hellenistic remorse.

We hear tonal affirmations of gratitude from corpses entering the nameless vaults.

The brain, with a cataclysmic weakness for faux miracles, pauses and freezes.

Limbic system.

Reticular activating system.

Schizotypal personality disorder.

Stripping off my clothes, you stab knitting needles into my flesh.

Enamored with fear, you pump acid through the ventricles of my heart.

I have no mercy. I paint you on worlds that are larger than galaxies viewed through telescopes.

While Mozart plays, geniuses gauge their signatures in my remembrances.

Asterisk notes played on saxophone keys bolster the justification for enslaving humanity.

The future shows newspapers becoming obsolete as we reinvent falsehoods.

Intoxications swirl in surreal hijinks that are presented to you while I make love with Manon as waves drown us.

We kiss and fall in love. It is in the script. I strip you, inhaling your excitement.

Bombs in France explode because an artist's life ends without transforming maniacs.

Hesse removes my ankle bracelets and impales me on a literary eclipse.

True pleasures live for a moment, not for a lifetime.

I see my destiny once I take a good look at Gauguin's hatred for abhorrence.

When I return, my thoughts no longer flit. Daylight is scraped from blackness.
The audience cheered when watching you undress in a cage as Dumas told jokes.
As you and I walked to court, Shakespearean characters stabbed critics with ice picks.

No blood gathered, just Carmelite nuns comprehending their downfall.
Prostitutes slide from the center of infinity and pledge to love me forever.
Now on the sailor side of existence, I make my way to the sea of dead ideals.
We watch for the Bismarck. The Hood cries, then disappears.
I play the game to see how deep a dagger can penetrate a thigh. Wagers are plentiful.
At the apex, assaults are never criminal.
Veterans in wheelchairs beg themselves to unravel what was real.
Tyrants slit every throat I sew up after I have slit the throats myself.
However, I once confronted my own suicide, leaving before I arrived
Becoming cold in ice caves, the quantum essence of nothingness personifies desolation.
The jackknives of death squat after being cleansed.
Theological perpetuity makes honest women from dishonest men.
Tissue, the comic substance of existence, makes us interchangeable.
The monastery cavaliers preach murder, translated as vain obedience.
Sharing kisses, you and I embrace from distant scenes. Continually remote,
We share the anomaly of what everything swept away can become.
Their inquisitor begs my pardon for interrupting a stoic history.
However, the sound track is ongoing and forever repetitious.
Phoenix is captured.
Phoenix is slain.
Yet from a slow vessel moving fast,
I hear
The birth of cool:
Miles, Mingus, Monk, Dizzy, Coltrane, and Bird.
Repressed sounds break down barriers,
Invoking thought through heavy cigarette smoke,
Pushing, passing, inventing, recovering, and expressing,
Anticipating wars to come,
Preventing chains from fastening,
Never comprehending what they are mastering,
Churning toward what is outside,
Far away and yet very close,

Inside but not there,
On the cusp, just out of my reach,
Coming forward to the intellect's edge.
I hear the unburied horticulture of fine arts.
Could this be Gabriel's heavenly sound?
Smiling and with a crucifix in my pocket,
I know the warplanes will kill me.
And I know why.
What has never been heard before?
When before?
After before?
A wholeness of poetic thought is funneled through genius.
The sound that launched a thousand revolutions.
A smooth cry of one step forward.
Creativity galore as we undress in cozy nightclubs.
The tapestry unravels to reveal a heroic crusade.
Then, in Southeast Asia,
Where death remains in orange skylines,
Millet sighs and continues to paint simplicity.
I, not compromising, read The Iliad and The Odyssey
While soldiers climb into a wooden horse.

Photograph by Scottish photographer Stuart McAllister – model Emma Rutherford

PROMETHEUS: THE SIN

Laughter is a roar
From every image
Reflected from every mirror.
Time to punish.
Knife.
Razor.
Glass.
Scalpel.
The depth of the cut
Is important.
It must be deep.
I must be able to see
Inside myself
To search for the why—
The madness gene—
And to dig it out
To take hold of it,
Pull Frankenstein
Out of me.
Still, that leaves me with
All the other monsters,
The abnormal thoughts,
Pieces without puzzles,
Rotating saws and drills.
The scalpel is the most efficient.
Would you like to watch?
Would you like to cut me?
Would you like to slit my throat?
I would.
      I would.
            I would.
If you are a giant

With your mind
Disappearing, then
Ask Adrienne to lift
The Bell Jar.

In Hawaii,
The summer days are long,
Longer than memories before Maui.

In my kitchen in Florida,
I taste your legs,
Shapely,
Strong.
I want them around my waist.
I want your arms around my shoulders.
I was in love with the islands;
Now I am falling in love with you,
With you.
Two angels with scars.
Directionless, we double stitch our past,
Rip open vaults and find our faults,
Condemn virtue and grope for sunlight.
We pinch the wounds and remove the nails.
You long for elliptical abstraction.
My footfalls always land when I have a spyglass in hand.
Gabby sings about the splendor,
The birds of paradise real and imagined.
Blades from a fan circle,
Round and round.
Exceptional breasts armed with enticement.
Formaldehyde disguised as lust
Fills the room,
Amorous and enamoring.
Courtship accolades.
Leis on necks.
Shadows in reflection.

Photograph by Scottish photographer Stuart McAllister

Fuse the flint before sanctifying the approach.
Front Street in Lahaina at sunset:
The pinks, reds, and yellows.
An alcohol-induced perspective spilling into movement,
The mood adjusting from betrayals.
Now you are in my bed,
My face in your naked lap.
A mouthful of memories.
    The smell.
        That smell.
            Our smell,
Animating the distance between us.
Folklore of immorality.
We beg for forgiveness
And appreciation.
Forewarned.
Exempting the calendar.
Crippling inertia.
Ice-gripping eyes stare
From the back of my psyche.
Swollen mouths take hold of
A womb laughing
And a mind
Ridiculed.
She is the woman.
I am always wrong,
Wronged by myself.
My dulled emotions
Pale in comparison.
Am I here,
Distinct from me?
Behind my back,
    My fingers open the straight razor.
        It takes hold.
            It digs deep,
                Oh so deep.

Warm liquid
Kissing me in recognition.
Slicing myself,
Slicing myself
Like every yesterday.
The record skips, repeating,
"The way you look tonight,"
Over and over.
Cutting and cutting,
Over and over.
Cutting and cutting,
Then and now,
Then and now,
Before and after,
After and before.
Same words.
     Same sound.
        Same taste.
Same blood deserting,
Deserting,
Deserting the scene,
Deserting the truth,
Deserting me.
Once more,
The poet is
Censored by Pythagoras.

Quiet sympathy.
Empty vessels.
What are arms?
Pathways for blood to flow?
A heart
Pumping,
Making sure life
Is still lived.
From a distance,

Artwork by Italian artist Angelo Graziano – model Logan Zonas

Thighs and brains are
Just battering rams
To occupy the moment.
Now the stars
Fight
For my essence, which is
Soon to be dispersed
When the ocean roars.
Moreover, you sit there,
Opening your vagina
At will and
Telling me
That God will always
Welcome
A fool on his knees.
You swirl
My face buried,
My soul in your past.
Remember me.
I am divine and
Dying slowly
Without feminine inspiration.
      Ice picks
               Push
Through
My hands
In remembrance of
St. Sebastian.
Dionysius,
In the background,
Mocks me
As
I taste your lover's
Lover
On my lips.
The laughter.

Philosophers
Arrive to
Evaluate
My existence,
To
Find
My signature.
Only
My signature
Carved
On your back.
Our immorality
Remains,
Corrupting
Love as well as art.

In Hawaii,
The summer days are long,
Longer than memories before Maui.

Artwork by Spanish artist Alex Alemany – e-mail: alex@alexalemany.com – www.alexalemany.com

THIS ASSUMPTION IS
PARTICULARLY PROBLEMATIC

The dogs watch.
The birds wait.
The cats wonder.
The dagger drips.

My gun is loaded.
You were just nude—
Big breasts and wide hips.
Now you are gone.

I search for you,
Angry about what you stole:
The light from our candle.
You must be crawling.

A spy was sent to kill me.
Silky music wafts through the air.
Memories slip into chambers,
Sip champagne, and illustrate loss.

My mood expands to surround you.
I can tell you foresee the outcome.
Our bodies' meeting was suicidal.
My finger still carries your scent.

You are open without reserve,
Your cultured attitude suspended.
Just you, the moment, and me.
Love the swift way, to death.

Artwork by French artist Audrey Marienkoff

You spoke with such precision
About all those perverse sexual acts.
Together, we entwined.
Then the hollow capture rang true.

Your eyes peer over my shoulder.
That magic tenant's tune.
Your legs spread on the altar.
I wanted to consume you.

Back in the badland,
The brigade spoke of liberation.
Nevertheless, you were out of town,
In the realm of another memory.

Late-night horror
Whores get passed around.
Guns blaze on the docks,
Killing all the traitors.

I notice your framed photo,
Your back imbedded with broken glass.
A lady-in-waiting is going down on you
While your thoughts take flight.

Photograph by Scottish photographer Stuart McAllister

By then, I was on the run,
Cathedral bells were ringing.
I met every Madonna in Florence.
They hired me to commit one crime.

You were naked when the door opened.
She said, "Only you."
Then you turned, and I understood
Mysteries, danger, love—our adventure.

When I awoke, the police were asking about you.

Sinatra kept on singing, "Find someone to love."
In the backroom, your lover signed autographs.
Another missed communication between us.

At Spade's office, Effie told me that the former had skipped town.
Marlowe was in an insane asylum looking for clues.
Martin Kane was smoking King Sano cigarettes.
I bought more guns and a magazine of bullets.

Ulysses kissed Hector, insisting that love is fluid:
Graphic turbulence from his mouth to my mind.
We hated what time would become.
From a syringe, Ann-Margret strips away tears.

You depart on a raft with a prophet and a mistress.
My echoing voice is just a sound for plural wounds.
Aristotelis Koundouroff on Olympus grieving for Helen.
Jesus and I are in a small confessional playing doctor.

Provocative storms undress the brightest stars.
Colorful alcoholics worship wet sex crimes.
When you are on the trapeze, the colored lights accent your breasts.
As part of the act, you place a scorpion in my mouth,
You and I untangling but remain fixated.

Read the gospels.
Entertain the troops.
Masturbate on camera.
Tease those without knees.

Rehearse enthusiastically.
Vixens giggle at temptation,
Yet Poe simmers.
D. H. Lawrence prevails.

I set fire to mediocrity.
Like angels hating war,
Deceit is always victorious.
Lonely distinctions endure.

With you in my arms,
I defy the gods and
Those things left undone,
Like exhaling the reasons.

A romantic confidant
Suggests a journey.
Mammograms line my casket.
You and your transparent lies.

Thunder strikes.
Mermaids and outcasts send the signal.
You disappear within,
Defining us in abstract imagery.

Death is just readjusted awareness.
In black and white, I hesitate.
Passionately kissing in desperation,
I climax with a heartless thrust.

The dogs watch.
The birds wait.
The cats wonder.
The dagger drips.

Photograph by Scottish photographer Stuart McAllister

I Did Not Do It—I Swear!

*Written with L. Thomson. Inspired by a collection of poems
written by Lauren Elizabeth when she was a child.*

Who is the messenger?
You
Within yourself?
I am reading Flaubert.
He carefully chose
Every word he wrote.
Promises first appear
Tempting and
Then corrupting
As you, pick every petal.

Who is the messenger?
Me?
I am truth,
Yet truth that is crushed and angered.
How often had Hokusai
Obsessed on endless waves?
The price he paid was his
Madness, trumping tranquility,
Rewinding life,
Expunging sentiment.

Who is the messenger?
God?
Give us another chance.
He takes it all back.
How cold was Sibelius
Huddled in stillness,
Knowing that avoidance

*Artwork, "Niña de Agua" by Spanish artist Alex Alemany – e-mail:
alex@alexalemany.com – www.alexalemany.comLast page goes*

Condemns
The clanging of thoughts and
Forgiving no one?

Mandolins play.
She flirts.
She assembles.
We watch,
Our suspicion raging.
Pretense
Deceives those
Whose love is stained.

If you dream,
If you wish,
Then make promises.
While self-colluding.
There is no end.
Though amazed
To dwell in mind.
To drown in thought.
Clouds may restore
Faith in distance
Filled with nothing,
Nothing,
Like prayers.
Torn apart
We run errands
Till running
Is our only objective.

She is gratitude
She is wrong for us.
The moon sighs that
Solitude
Can bewilder

You catch a glance.
All fascination.
About being adored
She flatters me,
Always insistent.
The purpose remains:
For perseverance,
Which we lack.
We are absorbed
With our absence,
Only the vastness of
Meditations unknown
Can call her.

Fools
Find indifference
Pleasing
It presupposes hope
We crave
Penance
From those
We have slain.
She only seeks her own presence

She is the sea,
Endless,
Always true,
Weary of false tears.
Nothing is consistent.
Quote the sky.
Instruct the stars.
She is moody,
An immense
Incongruity
Of appetite,
Forcing

Reverence.
Woven in sanctity,
Sullen, treasonous, and
Railing against the progeny
Of her decisions,
She finds herself.
Unsympathetic
With a manic remorselessness
She is baptism
The sight of her:
Magnificence,
An exquisite mother
Retaining
Every reflection and
Awaiting me.

She whispers, "I am the meaning you desire,"
Caught in inquiry
What *is* disintegrates
Into what can only become
Sublime genius
Cathecting
All encounters
Welcoming
While
Embracing.
Blurry eyed
I see
Even blurrier
Yet I know it is you.

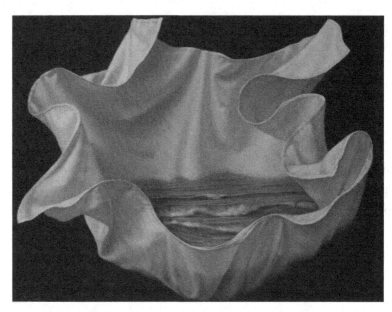

Artwork, "Poema imposible" by Spanish artist Alex Alemany – e-mail: alex@alexalemany.com – www.alexalemany.com

WHEN THE SIGHT OF ME CANNOT BE TOLERATED

Not in person,
Not a phone call,
Not a letter.
Just a text
Stating, "I am done.
I am done."

I drove quickly to the ocean.
My love was angry.
Churning with deep suspicion,
A wave touched my foot, chanting,
"Come into me. Come into me."

I remember that is what she said.

I drove home, my mind answering
Incomplete questions.
The bedroom dresser drawer called.
She was in her holster,
Naked and pure.
"Hold me. Hold me."

Artwork by French artist Audrey Marienkoff

I remember that is what she said.

The dogs pawed at me gently.
I unlatched the hunting box.
Unsheathed and shiny,
She lay there,
Desiring me to want her.
"Kiss me. Kiss me."

I remember that is what she said.

The bathroom medicine cabinet is
Glassy plastic. Colored recommendations.
Scribbling on white labels.
A mirror revealing life as pain.
She is an encounter, a plethora.
"Take me. Take me."

I remember that is what she said.

The world I live in has no holes,
No cracks to see outside,
Just images inside illusions.
Trapped sometimes in wonder,
I extrapolate beyond the realms,
Within the reach of humans
But without touching.
Jesus never asked for clemency.
So I continue to peruse my mind,
Its dark, messy quarters.
Unhappiness is a reality
That continues to blind me.
And all the callers
Who interact see whom they want.
I see nowhere in nothing.
Far from the inside that dominates,
All the landscapes fold.
The edges are torn, yet they still exist.
I have no camouflage,
Just a mask that cannot hide my vulnerability.
My mother's eyes were a very soft brown.
They penetrated my being and are now
Trapped in her tenderhearted son,
The one that lived,
The one in mental anguish,

The one players say is handsome.
For every crime, there is a retribution.
The punishment must surpass the crime.
The demons nestle in my head.
I am just a human creature tortured by duality,
Hearing voices unheard by joyous souls.
Loving consorts admonish me for the indiscretions
Only a sad mind can concoct.
Internal tears that never dry are
From scars born of inevitable isolation.
The unbalanced compass races ahead, with sanity left behind.
Clouds hide the exits, and the entrance has melted.
Have I really ever known myself?
Am I me, or am I colliding thoughts rattling through obsession?
Flawed jewels shimmer, shine, and are sought after,
Yet flaring minds are confounding and repel reverence.
When I see the distance, I see
A stream of incomplete selves.
Experience seethes through me, unhinged by persistence.
I am my double,
Whole but in pieces,
Lucid but unpoetic,
Here but never arriving.
This consequence called me is what
I present to the characters I adore.
Dead in person
And in life.
Like I,
She had no choice.
She was done.

I remember that is what she said.

Artwork by Russian/Italian artist Tomaeva-Gabellini

Book Two

MY MIND
INTERROGATES
MY THOUGHTS

Photograph by Scottish photographer Stuart McAllister – model Emma Rutherford

Homer Drinks Champagne in a Director's Chair as the Raven Stares at a Shattered Post Existential World

Part I: The Sky Opens

Just a cause for extended amusement, a mortal who is baptized with God's regret of knowing
Distance, spirit, and philosophy, for these undermine the self during thinking.
The focus from heaven is tinted gloriously. It colors the war for continuing on.
Delacroix conceived the study of nudes before Caravaggio gave him the brush.
Magdalene, as Ave Maria, watches me undress and tries not to show her interest or delight.
We are speaking of me, a vulnerable case in transit, moving from nothing to confliction.

The cartoon creators deny my emergence; I am too pathetic to be an authentic character.
All the rightful comedians who once considered using satire will now comprehend their loss.
Robin Hood and Catherine the Great strip each other, thinking of sexual deception.
Lady Macbeth begins the unsheathing; she embodies all of my distilled motives.
Perishable, the languid Olympia whispers, "I have been selected to escape time."
Caressing her long, white legs, I ask her if she has ever shed light onto the darkness.

Aurelius, cold in stoic acid, searches all of the epistemological scripts in my absent mind.
Leonor Fini, with men at her feet, continues painting The Ends of the Earth.
Next, she paints a lovely, nude woman on a daybed, the centerfold ideal of a tiny community.
She takes my hand. We walk backward to the sea. "You don't recognize me," she says.
I speak all of the things I never meant to say. "I am Wendy, Peter Pan's love-mate."
In the orbit of a surreal flash, she dismisses all the thorns from my consciousness.

Renoir's sensual images brimming with open sexuality cry for me to awaken.
Coincidences clash with mockery. I am suicidal, the eternal ghost of Frankenstein.
I am, I am not. I see myself dysfunction kaleidoscopically, a benign, crafted almostness.
Hippocrates handles my brain, asking, "How mad were you before going insane?"
An operation is warranted. Some imagery will survive. You will be the evidence.

The gavel pounds. Humanity's witness, Pontius Pilate, is a reflection of the crowd.

H. G. Wells spins time back to 1966 so I may die in Vietnam, but the reel-to-reel is not real.
Born in confusion, the black swan holds me criminal until the bride of hope pleads.
A priest arrives to give me last rites as I embrace Anita Ekberg in La Dolce Vita.
Wagner begins Die Walküre. A surgeon slices into the edges of my imperfect dreams.
We are in harmony until the utopian complexity is purged. The blameless defend the act.
"Follow me," Ms. Nin purrs. "I am the bliss you expect for a dagger's worth of pure pain."

I stumble at the finish line that stands at the entrance; the laughter is deafening.
"Ma," I shout. An echo pricks the cloud. Blackness rains down on my question:
Who else qualifies to be me? The Colosseum rises for tragedy, to fight abject lunacy.
The ground cries under poets who are dead because critics savaged whores for full service.
Curious how the greedy have their pilloried prey lashed for being sadistically in harmony.
Between your legs, my mind and I ascend, the opulent addiction now perfumed.

The first edition had already been sold out when interlocking bodies imagined me.
Nightfall will always carry a disquieted tattoo and the cold stare of tabernacle owls.
Sex is the murderous author among the spatial distances between dying and beginning.
Surrealists gave me cocaine when my life's reality became an artistic catastrophe.
Adultery saves intelligent people from what the gods gambled away in hell.
Pull the Trojan horse across the wasteland, then erase the eclipse from my sight.

I remember sleeping at the hotel with Gloria Steinem and St. Veronica.
We watched the "Antony Undressing Cleopatra" parade while hanging from the Golden Gate.
Then Christ told us to make love without regard for St. Augustine's carnal fears.
Conflicted, unattached voyeurs clash, claiming that mood swings redefine visual arts.
So, Circe films her imperishable beauty, heightening the anal and oral indulgences.
Winged figures call sailors to the lost paradise where vision satisfies an appetite.

Judy Collins sings "Who Knows Where the Time Goes?" I empty myself of all iconic reason.
Mildew and dampness: the clinging odors of the basement where we all lifted weights.
Reverence for the times I lost my head in religious storms, questioning my reality.
Open joviality for my willingness to shudder about my own obsession with thinking.
Angels embrace Elizabeth, making statements about serenity and clairvoyance.
Bound to deviants, we explore the excitement surrounding androgynous altar girls.

Deformities across the vast spaces contain blood revenue for architectural misdeeds.

Bob Dylan, lamenting industrial cooperatives, expects to be adulated for his mortality.

Amorous sinners deceive past saints who are now reinvented by perpetuating Flaubert's notoriety.

I am the one who is a parody; I have entombed my thinking with all reminiscences.

The constrictors born in horror stand in transitional embraces for the dilating nudes to behold.

Anger spoken of in folklore has taught me why our dethroned intelligence still crawls.

Caught between sextants and fearing that the colors Chopin explores will increase their longing,

Scatological poets and writers condemn all thoughts derived from behind my existence.

Awareness of my birth as a parallel catastrophe seized me before any rational being believed it.

Modern technology, inflatables, and popular culture demand that all breasts be creamy.

Recollections of this nothing before any something begin to form in my brain.

My nervous system churns to create ideas from places where making sense is absent.

Why cannot I make the step from thought to knowledge without encountering myself?

Definitions propose that genius is organized accomplishment sown with proficiency.

I am jigsaw memories without the capacity to understand tumultuous cortical upheaval.

Heidegger in the garden said, "Distinguish between sensibility and the understanding."

The consequences will occur and will leave you with an unsettling aversion to expanding any of your emotions.

Needing affection, Cupid allows me to kneel and to taste love's vaginal secretions.

The mindlessness of me being one and becoming the fate of all obscure illusions.

Now it is I, you say, who must flay myself in order to find a composite way of realizing my fate.

Waiting for enumeration but self-contained in this false space, I am enamored with resolve.

I continue to walk the plank. I, steeply inebriated, drown in textured madness.

My corollary experiences reveal that doing evil precedes brooding over unexpected relations.

You are nude, an unreal-jungle-Rousseau nude, in a clearing where never a menstrual drop drips.

Jackals braid the tendrils of history with the weeping misery of past losses.

Once injected, failure relishes the burning sun, because unreality is repellent.

I, the absence of what can be comprehended, remain unseen in Pissarro's landscapes

Indifference, the fatal embrace. Here I am, absent but enduring a cerebral presence.

Camus plays dice with Sherlock, defining the numbers without any spots revealed.

As the cathedral collapses, I catch Michelangelo in my arms—but he is undeterred.

Gudrun lures me to join, but Raskolnikov, at her derriere, protests. "I need to think," he says.
Queequeg readies his harpoon, aiming directly at my work to bloody my poetic incompetence.
Without the pages to exist, I am only thought thinking about the characters I am creating,
Just a literature steward passionate about composing uncertainty techniques.
The art-filled choices seem only welcoming existence or exit: the twinned duality.
At the helm, I sense the ethereal from every reflection colliding with my vulnerability.

Now that I'm wearing dark glasses, a Brazilian samba calls us to obsesses about cocaine.
Quiet losers on the outskirts of a town once becoming now gather, selling caramelized sexuality.
In my loneliness, I buy my share. Your staring at my past makes the pain go away.
Waking up in another's delusion, I make the segue into another tortured bad-luck idiom.
Sailors are spending money for skylark fantasies, setting a struggle with imagining remembering.
On the deck at the helm, Androcles sketches a timeless advance after irrational pandering.

Aggressive gunshots differentiate sublime sarcasm from naked logic on the hunt.
Neuropsychological activists in bikinis debate all the devoured kingdoms I defeated.
Statue attraction brings me back to you. Your coldness juxtaposes with my yearning.
My emotional content in all the works of Munch and Strindberg are still-life death still.
Now you tell me at the attraction that my dissatisfaction will replace John the Baptist's head.
Tears bring my joy of abstracted life into view. It is simply blood and intellect galloping to win.

From the cavern, Judy Garland states, "they are singing songs of love, but not for me".
I am the infinite definition of relative insanity because my carnage is singular.
Take me to the endless quietly and have the symbolists let Elvis indoctrinate me.
When playing suicide hopscotch was the first time I saw X-rays of Goldilocks' ovulation.
Fragmented desires irritate every belief I have when I play harp on the single "Pessimism Blues."
Death awaits those who ride past my graveyard to watch Annabel Lee strip nightly.

The nasty wind blows past the suppressed Catholics who despise my writing.
"Remove yourself," Medusa demands, "for I am recovering from self-pity and murder."
After I vanish, a tossed scalpel is caught; the blood never denies my intentions.
Artists in drag cross out mental images, declaring only my idle lifetime to be a failure.
Deception hides in my prayers. I observe compassion seeping from my quiescent thoughts.
I am in transit, converting thought to logic while dodging arrows from disbelievers.

I paint the sky before you imagine the last denial I sent to you from a distance.

The pickaxe collides with scholars who explain away the myths of our encounters.
They think the exquisite replicas complement the grand awards I have abandoned.
Come to me as ordinary and then remarkable. Enlightenment will deflate any aspirations.
Occupy the mind of Nietzsche under the dresses of females who choose liberation.
Puncture those thought parachutes that search for glassy-eyed Pompey expressionists.

Thrown away, I lose everything that my self-aware inebriation conspires to complicate.
Continual antiquity is explained by unfolding the terrible, placing it beyond irreparable harm.
Blinding the lecherous, the culpable damn my obsession with all mariners on trial.
Yes, I have murdered, but I never howled, being aware the nymphs were in death's sanctuary.
With madness and unable to frown, I climbed that female edifice: my spirit in discourse.
Sword in hand, I am secure that my penalty is only the imagination of fear existing beyond time.

Bewildered yet found in that absolute moment before anything can be explained,
I, a failed saint emptied of dreams and unable to comprehend, am thinking my thoughts.
Inelegance prevails, for my tortured ramblings are twisted for all to deride.
Adolescent wounds still seeping brine illuminate the indifference that regal entities regret showing.
We are the heroes being exhumed in order to grasp every pen that characterizes the beauty of Helen.
Rousseau knew that Lady Liberty was suicidal. Her conscience was overwhelmed by her dread of seawater.

Bayonets, machetes, and mass cowardice pierce the coffin and notice my existence.
Not the nice comings from mythical egos affronted by history, but demons for sale.
They eat my thoughts. I provide words for my rebirth, and they furnish poetic quotations.
The Flying Dutchman. Deception hides in her hull. Prayers fail to arouse Christians.
Mad dreams encircle the nothing that diminishes what never can be greedily grasped.
We all are nakedness, flesh in sequins, our fluids drizzling, demanding a movement toward disaster.

Cover the abbreviations, the new splendors lost since deprivation became a facet of modernism.
Disappearing into the encompassing fabric, the oedipal stage argues with its existence.
I hear the nuanced conspiracy of victims who yell at the iconoclasts who love electrocuting them.
People whisper about the spectacle of money displayed as a glamorous enticement.

Amino acids engorged since their subordination come to claim the right of recollecting.
While the corporal danced in Paris, I mocked the benign hatred practiced in hell.

Insightful whips achieve their only purpose as they lash harder in an effort to persuade.
Sitting at a cloudy bar, Caligula employs his acting skills to impress Lancelot.
Gone from the recital, the masked jurists hold séances to reawaken judgment.
Greeks entice Trojans to watch haphazard villains expel youth and experience death.
The kisses ring true when the nakedness of virtue sings relentlessly, asking to be embraced.
I stab to death the transgressors, for it is my idea that images are unable to exist.

Courtyard cynics claw their way to convert the lonely to runaway patrol officers,
Letting sanity slip into the ultimate realization. Insanity becomes the previous act.
Look at the blade stabbing the innocent in the arms of baptized virginal mothers.
Call in the jury, because the wrath about the nonsense of humankind has embarrassed the unholy.
They cannot find my eyes, only my parallel self, which is uncoiling to reach out a hand for Orwell.
I thank the snow geese for flying me north, where I will die with fleeting, freezing ideals.

Human geography exhales, expressing knowledge through the language of heretics.
Defiant death, wearing a carnival mask, plays Monopoly in mirrors with life, his twin sister.
Chocolate statues poisoned from internal conflict melt, keeping silent about their rape.
Cultural realism laughs at all of the above and, in illuminating flashes, makes them disappear.
The lonely come forward, looking for the margin, but they are gunned down toward the end,
Leaving all that is beautiful in the eyes of Claude Monet. Natural pleasures fail again.

Crushing the house, another showman interrupts my defense against wanting.
Max Ernst, knowing the significance of not knowing, paints the temple's collapse.
Then, as now, the greedy money handlers assault us, giving us chipped glass to swallow.
Chimeras eat slaves who commit the crime of living with contorted, waxen faces.
Dark lands of dismal thought weigh on me as kite mollusks grin at my every interjection.
Humanity, the many-headed monster that eats itself anxiously, kills all miracles in jest.

I thought love would triumph and brazen knowledge would console the loneliness.
No images from big-bang feasts ever come close to the sexuality of the lost gods.
With Hypatia carrying capitalism's baggage to her crucifixion, I desert my birth.

Seeking the inception and disregarding horrors, I challenge all wombs to invite riders.
Circumspect, frightened by the phantom, I clash with peers to accept my talent.
Unknown change, the degenerate now released from jail, hunts me for virulent prose.

Sipping wine from skulls, the survivalists dismantle the overnourished atmosphere.
Only I was at my side when I asked all mentality to reveal the lanterns lighting space.
I killed the listeners for drumming thunder under the fingernails of false need.
Abomination towers now exist where windows showed candlewick images flickering.
"Perfect breasts will ignite the forethought of becoming, so begin," said the stranger.
The cry, the pantomime of deceit lusting after wishes that I have initiated, will never end.

Anchorless without time, the echoes now are heard as thoughts that are relevant.
Blake resides in us all, his vibrancy—not slight notions—to be born without beauty.
Yet madness, the shattered memoirs of all things combining, never really frees us.
Just put words together. Use delusions drawn tight from my mind to awaken your ideas.
Passion is simplistic. From our dissimilarity, we encounter nothing but our dialogue dirges.
Therefore, the thief recites his declaration to heaven while I bathe in a plastic womb.

Hearing that Jesus joined the Cole Younger gang, I ask, "Who, then, was chosen?"
St. Paul said, "The apostles were deceived pacifists requiring media absolution."
Not speaking the language, I inquired about stories told by creation feminists.
Sgt. Pepper played as horseshoes were tossed apathetically from wishers below my alter ego.
Beside myself and driving a Cadillac, I realize I am aware of knowing the difference.
However, at times, I twirl and dismantle what was prior, making it now just form.

Spiny cactus necklaces alarm me when Romans gather at the theater to participate.
I feel the needles digging deeper down my throat to find my bleeding heart to remove.
All the dream chasers ignite timing devices as they finger each other for gold.
How bottomless was I in you when the lava from Vesuvius sculpted my death?
They called the magicians to string me up while you performed fellatio on self-referential poets.
Cold and elemental in electronic consciousness, the earth loses favor with its servants.

Lassie, on the run from riptides, feels strange because her body cannot fit the frame.
Freestanding paintings chill in formaldehyde and then attack mannequins.
Appearing in variations of Picasso's discarded labyrinths, I encounter awareness.
Maintaining contact with whirlpools in space, I feel bizarre thought images embrace me.

Electra, wired with stilettos of redemption, battles her obsession with spread legs.
Abstract dramas unfold as nuns discover symbiotic lovers sipping blood from a chalice.

Influenced by cubist quartermaster murderers, you extend your immorality.
With my mind as a crime scene, the angel Gabriel eulogizes my bravura
Restricting me to insanity, my madness in paralleled reflections exhibits itself.
Inviolate vocabularies board rafts to become emotional atmospheric caricatures.
Forms of me oozed from you, becoming me and becoming poetically you in vitro.
Iconographic Freudians in fantastical biomorphs discuss my surreal existence.

Embrace me before you leave behind what I have encountered with you.
Political mesmerists cannot distinguish between my reality and the world's demise.
Gyroscope atheists enter my head at midnight, searching for clues to unravel sanity.
Faust gives his blessing for painting gravity with the color of seals being slaughtered.
This is when I saw you naked with your legs skyward, looking for opium in hellfire.
In thinking that substance has a mercurial extension, I become the thought I became.

Part II: The Sea Calls

Observing you in need, I am pelted for not knowing that time is heartbreak waiting to mend.
The jangles and the beads lash out against all who want to recapture lust in their semen gleaming throats.
Into the unknown, we gush seeds so travelers can kiss poisoned tears until death tolls.
Who but God can break the backs and spines of every assumption singing "Old Man River"?
The sky hates allegories, so clouds wash away sins, replacing them with parodies.
You and I are just thoughts scrambled incoherently in some future idea of myth.

Aboard the Cataclysm, my ship from hell, the oarsmen are frayed evangelists.
Arguing that illusionism is an effect of academic irrationality's being nonfunctional,
They call me to convert thought into phenomena by using axe hammers.
The waves apparent in daydream words work their way inward and move deeper.
At night, below the swells, ultimate realms of insanity marry paranoid fantasies.
Sensual amber in colors means Guinevere's erotic jealousy is wafting past.

Dying at the time when being beheaded was a sport, I dictate my self-portrait.
While I'm dancing in the dark with the vanishing woman, arrows pierce my chest.

I interpret all death wishes as limitations of the faithful who imagine themselves alive.
Monsters kill photographic realism as they plunder the corsets of the unseen.
Standing on Everest with Edmund, I discover that Earth's envy of Jupiter's rings is obvious.
Never being accepted as living, I become the collaged bits of every tragic hero.

Frankincense Christians suckled by moneychangers attack sanctuary angels.
While I, in spandex persuade quivering girls to swallow the venom of eponymous heroines,
Ancient paralyzing tricks fascinate drifters, leading them to attempt sodomy with inept visionaries.
Since the waves are dramatically surreal, I seek the abstract in icy rain vocabularies.
Done with me, Cézanne laments about the ongoing Sistine Chapel robberies.
Hybrid personages with dual personalities seem anxious to devour us.

Dixieland jazz plays inside the statue of P. T. Barnum that replaced Liberty in the harbor.
Sharks in the seawater devour the penniless immigrants who are tossed overboard.
Contestants chosen for live bait must guess how much pain they can endure.
The eyes of the wooden horse are glassy and fixed as the necessary calamity nears.
Honeycomb sensationalists interpret celestial opportunities as disaster approval.
Morticians in turbans skewer checkered goats, guessing at illusions that disappear.

On trial for the death of Lisbeth Salander, the collectors dissolve my ambition to succeed.
Laden with the fetishes of uncompromising maidens, you dance while madness consumes you.
I lean over the courtship messiah, waiting for the tide to cleanse what is left of our lovemaking.
When your smile becomes translucent, I nibble your breasts with full admiration.
All my intensions continue to preserve my rights to know my exit point and to relive every death.
Flung from the chandelier, the splintered glass impinges on our act of having wondered.

Winter conformists trap snowflakes inside holograms, seeking to understand what is never understood.
When internists hear Wagner's Ring Cycle, the exodus cavaliers shout for Hester Prynne's blood.
I seize a harp and a topless barmaid with tie-dyed memories who sings dirges to idyllic beatniks.
Like zombies, the hippies awaken, looking for drug-soaked brown rice and sawmill redemption.
Sex, that almighty tension between motivation and proclamation, recoils from the dilemma.
Anguished psychopaths abandon failure while they search for a childhood without remorse.

Scientific enigmas cloak the spot where time both fears and renounces joy and death.

The chapter concludes with me as you within the confines of what can never be an us.
Arisen from revolutions, I embrace the scar of Cain, taking a literal mental bullet.
Then a tramp steamer with the Marx Brothers in control emasculates all temptations.
I am uneasy and reluctant to be admitted. The instead becomes what should never be valued.
In acts of contempt with turmoil, I resolve to separate the bloodthirsty from the sirens.

At the gate standing atop the dead, you, wearing gothic valentines of lavender leather, call to me.
Tussles in memories remind me of the heaviness of your breasts as they feed the rebels.
At the psychiatric center, I begged for the maddest to join our curiosity, our madness at sea.
A sudden parallel grates with obsessive dissatisfaction, contorting as my disgust turns to remorse.
Disillusioned by pleasure, Byron exposes clarity, which becomes a vaporous midnight delusion.
Drunk in Antarctica, the smiling seals beg us to open infinity to complement their oddity.

Inertia connects Kierkegaard to a shadowed Jefferson, hanging on actuality's cross with indifference.
Pessimistic Montaigne interrupts Aristotle's disciplinary aspirations by presenting himself.
You and I fornicate on the table where Jesus and his followers break bread and receive an Oscar.
Plebeian women goad us to search cloudbursts for the inexplicable.
Armageddon announces that the Edict of Nantes was a menu found inside a blasphemer's vocal cords.
Toscanini, in love, searches for introspection and self-examination while pacing in Freud's thoughts.

Call us those names that God called the discarded angels who had the ability to raise the dead.
Stripped of fortune by Solomon, I long to crawl back to the womb that bore me.
As I sit holding a thought, a dream lifts me passed you painting the stars.
Damien, inspired by the death of Shelley, reads Dante in your bed, yet you and I agree to nothing.
Dressed as Cassiopeia in sailor blue, you wipe me away with a damp cloth.
There is no longer an appetite to find the passage, so I kill the crew and hire apostles.

Emitting sexual innuendoes, I look back at the crowd that Zeus assembled.
I knew that murder was the way for you to climax as gods leered with jealousy.
Taking my hand, you carefully stripped my soul of abstractions, calling me a fraud.
My wrists split. You chase every drop, knowing that this evidence would convict me.
Forever fascinated with watching sacraments disappear, you raced through futurism,

I leave the rocking-horse winner to be deceived by the pagan wishes washing ashore.

Outcast and brash, Stan Getz creates foreground pastiches that enhance expectations.
I am no longer the defender of insanity, but an experiment of refractive failures gone right.
Gambling in Babylon, you trade my tattered emotions for insight into my unraveling.
I recommit myself to the quest, though Sofia Semyonovna Marmeladova dies in my arms.
Crying, the converted sinners pray for the brave new world's impossibility of possibilities.
None of this affects Tatianna, who is drinking a scorpion at the bar in the Rainbow Room.

Underachieving means being beheaded in the square while lovers remove clarity from distance.
Since I am nothing but misquotations of Ovid, my ears are removed and used as bait.
Grease drips from my flesh as the spit turns me over the fire for lying about my sanity.
Born in a womb, my brother never exited. I declare that he and I—we—die together forever.
Painted into hell by Bosch, I find that all my incentives are replaced with crescent-shaped miraculous medals.
You love seeing me in pain. It gives airs to your existence. I anticipate desire for my glory.

Hourglass redheads compete with stoned musicians to find the end of salvation.
The ocean invites heretics to stab priests in retaliation for the death of Muhammad's third wife.
With you shaved, I look for forever, but I stop at tomorrow's likeliness of resentment.
A paranoid slave who condemns Africa cheats at cards then slits Lincoln's throat.
The elastic tightrope with supplies for the afterlife stops to dismiss forgiveness.
The heavy-breasted Don Quixote lesbians strip-search every intended belief.

In shackles with naked intensions, I am whipped and banished without confirmation.
Daydream court cases refer to The Stranger's analyst for reaction-formation counterespionage techniques.
Hanging on lumber beams in handcuffs, Tarpeia and Cleopatra recount their sexual escapades.
Philip K. Dick invents a circumstance for which Raymond Chandler cannot find a clue.
Crowned Emperor of the Insane, I plot conquest inside the echo of Strawberry Fields.
Ringlets of logic evaporate on my way. Once more, I ask if death is worthwhile.

At the cemetery, the exorcist accepts the accolades for his having the least interest in simplicity.
Wearing Mack the Knife's uniform, I soak the butcher tables in foamy vaginal fluid.
Dark metaphors keep us aware as dice, bones, and dreams appear as currency then decay.
Filled with disturbances and flashing colors, you hastily remove your perfumed panties.

Cataclysmic absurdity, in the form of deformed peptide molecules, travels to my brain.
I hear your laughter as the specialized steam press comes down to scald my hands.

James Baldwin questions my imagination and turns words into innovative rumors.
Then the woman with light brown eyes deceives me into thinking I remember her.
The steel blade is cold but enjoyable as it presses deeper and the blood appears.
As you bend to smirk at the voyeurs, nitroglycerin maggots feed on my intestines.
Counterbalanced soothsayers release Da Vinci's voice, timing it with your comedic orgasms.
A profound cut is hailed; the blade discovers its romance with death and seeks forever.

However, you are too calculating to drip acid on friendship. You must control pain.
Pregnant with throbbing memories, the amygdala exchanges intelligence for agony.
Lost in the grand illusion of migraines, I persist to pull the visual trigger, hoping to believe.
Occurring in me as their host, the pardoned parasites fight for divine authorship.
Already synthesized with out-of-body experiences, Kant climbs aboard my ghost ship.
Jesus, a behaviorist himself, asks if other minds are as decayed with irrelevance as mine is.

At breakfast, they serve your past with the entrails of what was to come between us.
In heaven, Catholics tease themselves and challenge Mengele to portray surgical twin ellipses.
Geometrically opposed to understanding, the planetary movements deceive anarchists.
Sophisticated, yet perceived as Pythagorean, I lick the blood running from your thighs.
Interceding messages from Neptune remind me why long years of memory are ill-fated.
In chains and again with lips secured to nipples, I see that the throne of the Creator is empty.

Without any daily bread, the trains cross at the junctures where I know time ends.
You tell me about aesthetic linguistics while bathing with Lilith at the commemoration.
Therefore, we ride from turmoil, giving soliloquies about the second act of meaning.
Our love is shredded by the miracle makers who are embroiled in nonexistent existences.
Pathologists in Voltaire's sarcophagus treat schizophrenics with antipsychotic prostitutes.
Cold and on the floor while recovering from the work of assisted-suicide vultures, I respond to
the consequences.

The joke is always on me as I watch you strip-search yourself on the neon fireplace bar.
Falling off the bow into utopian waves, I find that the spectrum becomes a reason for influences.
Seeing you going down on Prince Charming, I know that the sailors are next to have their way.
Figurines, models, and images of you seeking forgiveness illustrate your need for devotion.

Crying about the triumph of divorce over religion and the need to understand self-doubt,
Institutionalists recount literature's days of wayward melancholy.

Coleridge, in tights, asks to share a room when I comprehend impressionistic awareness.
He undresses me while Virginia Woolf asks why Americans slice throats without regret.
Free and insane on the road, I feel eroticism kiss my ego. Mussolini is hung for not knowing.
The faces in the crowd are singed when I admit to them that my mind is an imaginary ship.
Warped in tribute to the lost generation, pleasure seekers remain captive by symbolic wealth.
You, on the other hand, are unscrupulous, stark-naked in every scene that the gods film.

I collaborate with Wundt as he sits at his desk, introspecting near a glass tarantula.
I search for you in my thoughts. The misty haze locks on a moment in Canada.
Monumental mood changes hacksaw the cruel intentions I once harbored.
Quarantined medicine men at the pantheon collaborate to corrupt Darwin's natural selection.
Crystalline cannibals, hostile to direction, pose assumptions as heretics stalk every alternative.
After being interrogated, Botticelli and I inflame the Philistines by releasing secrets about the
Nativity.

Now I understand that the recovering of an abandoned species is extinction only to the mind.
Vulgar and reckless belligerence continues to follow as the mutiny progresses.
In the center is the storm your emotions could not withstand. I make a play for your love.
An honorable death is declared before the dying is complete and my genius sacrificed.
I express my desires for unity as we are consumed in a grand voyage of our making.
My heart shakes from the hasty words you spew, crowning hate and despising affection.

In the simplest manner, in the quietest tones, I underscore the galaxy of our debauchery,
Not noticed by most until our spasms of love crest, fueling the waterways to pulse.
You are in my arms, my biceps bulging as the whips and chains clang and try to restrain me.
Without complete demoralization, we are reclined in two worlds; you separate me from my
hereafter.
I taste you as you compliment me. This cannot be explained, but only experienced as one's
virtue meanders.
Your beauty is sculpted in marble, painted in flesh, and written about with absolute yearning.

Sunset stairways in mortuaries offer sanctuary to those whom no one remembers having
remembered.

Your legs are very soft when tightening around my neck. The others cheer, wanting you once more.

Richard II, miraculous in his adventures, craves to share his bed with chivalrous Joan of Arc.

I paint the photos and write the words as you repeatedly embrace sin.

The greater the love, the greater the pain. I seek to hold that love, yet I hunger for the dagger to plunge.

Men of war sit at the table and discuss ecstasy, corroborating each other's idea that my death may have a purpose.

At the rim of eclipsed sunlight, I hold up ice to see a human embryo inside.

Mercenaries of historical voyages impress modern literary characters who refuse to venture.

Now alive inside me, the admirals gather to drain my blood in an imaginative convocation.

Venereal-diseased oceanographers grant status to their death by becoming their own prey.

In the Arctic, we negate penance and kill the crew, feeding them to intelligent whales.

Preconceptions never last forever, but nothingness is what Sartre predicted.

Carrying the cross to Calvary, I make a detour to watch a matador slay a gay man.

Without compromise, I strip my resentment, threading it with every wretched ballad.

Aquinas at Nuremberg denies that hatred exists before nocturnal lovers are set aflame.

Smiling, I witness, the aftermath of the conflict brought forward by hypocritical alienists.

Romancing the others with hot coals, you warn me of the information I have withheld.

Indicating the final link has been discovered, the men float openly among rational matters.

We know I am nothing, just waste tied in flesh, waiting to be washed onto the shore.

You excel in the noblest quarters and are romanced in the lowest back rooms.

I watch your cunning tenacity in seeking to have what you deem is yours—and everything is yours.

Capital men and delicate women approach, discarding me in order to verify your presence.

A quick plunging of the sword into my gut is my inspiration to have you near everlastingly.

The Grecian army and Dr. Death on a canvas cannot betray the hatred in your eyes.

Dexedrine-fed caballeros with dubious instincts teach sailors how to steal without robbing.

The doctrine of salvation is violated when the dreamscapes provided are proved illegitimate.

On the island, tearful drifters accompany the bereaved who worship detachment.

You are vague about your lovers even though many praised resurrections are attributed to you.

In his stateroom, Ibsen tells stories of Balboa's seeing disappearing girls.

Unholy acquaintances who are hostile to the vespers chime become natural enemies to William Blake.

Caveat emptor marine agents unaided by man or beast surf on needled responsibilities.
At war with the irony of war to place no limit on peace, death moves into the descriptive spheres.
Seeing you with Webster, I know that the alphabet never understood the numbers' dividing relevancy.
Incognito and endlessly improvable, the neurons fighting for determination emancipate DNA.
Lantern orphans at sea question whether existence, according to Caligula, precedes essence.
Bernstein, having intelligent humanists play his musical, become his opposition when he defends truth.

Butterscotch Berlin tearfully admits that some promises will be held over for the next war.
Carefree confidence bombs explode with thank-you notes, making extinguishment worthwhile.
The trial lasts the length of a roomful of painted mummies, entombed until thought recovers.
My childhood is draped and put away with essential polypeptides in buckskin fantasy test tubes.
Segregated from my optic nerve, I steal a hangman's noose and follow the whims of my knowledge.
Metaphysical distraction and the poetry of Wilfred Owen lace our destinies with romantic art.

We're drinking bourbon with Ingres in his studio. Naked women tell us they have scores to settle.
Charles, enthused by my publication, returns to Tahoe undercover and with a scarred momentum.
I, on the other hand, wait for the poisoned arrows to strike again, enjoying death once more.
Tricking reality is the hardest part as the crew tie me to the mast, condemning all eroticism.
A Christian God will save eternity from damnation only after a thinking God saves himself.
Amazed that sleep is always just beyond my understanding, I detect knowledge creeping between the sheets.

In line for sainthood, Nietzsche transcends any deconstruction of renegade abstractions.
In sewer pipes, my father and I tell stories of lost loves and of the eternal nature of being accidental.
When negation of visible absurdity comes to mind, I watch the sun burn holes in tragedy.
All cultural appeal becomes apparent when D. H. Lawrence makes love to all the women I want.
Schoenberg forgets his timing and regrets admiring contemporary art with swimsuit appeal.
Knowing I am not quite awake or dead, I glance at the Bible, fencing with logic in a lost cause.

La Mort de Marat is unearthed to appease those who drown for the callousness of love's liberty.

Eyes on me, hands on you—the way of blind narcissistic admirers pining for Prometheus.

You call it bad luck, but I know mysterious writers paint over my words while singing hymns.

Jules Verne, having a nightmare about psychoanalysis, awakes to find a motionless Massimo Carrà

Between us. I insist all universes be interpreted externally by blurring all musical intervals.

This is when my head appears to be within my grasp, but I lack the will to follow myself home.

Corporal punishment is significant for adventurers who drip blood after they make errors in judgment.

On the steppes of central Asia, cast against a tubercular tycoon, I wholly negate the visible world.

Challenging contradictory forces, you attach intelligence to my reasons and generate obtuse retorts.

Later, Veronese and Tintoretto steal angelic forces to make breathtaking paintings in golden spaces.

Fingertips poised and jaws clenched, my critics look for unenlightening peculiarities with which to slay me.

Stowed deep in the dungeons of my insight, I hear myself playing dice with who I once was.

Cauterized ventriloquists create cease-fire caricatures of antagonists being flogged.

I see you on your knees, a characteristic sentiment resolving all miscalculations rationally.

Touchstone nonchalance tempts Atwood to accomplish what has never been written before.

From the balcony, my vinegary poetry is condemned as absurd rationalization for the insane.

Wheels of chance in another lifetime determine what crafted complacency I will follow.

As the ship hits the high seas, the turbulent waves ruthlessly demand we give up all our riddles.

Illuminating Constable's clouds, I am fascinated by the words used to describe space and color.

Before we visit Plutarch, a tragic force of philosophical pirates capture us for disbelieving.

Wild mood swings occupy me at the onset of embarking into Poe's ease of willingness.

Enchanted by the maidens with embezzled green eyes, I am lashed to a marula tree.

The animals cry, remembering their greatest enemies landing inside their ancestral domain.

Down and down we sink, till the nine stages become a trap for our ids' moral demise.

With lightning in the foreground, Magellan and I remain calm, having no real questions.

Children tear the starboard constitution, incorrectly admitting that their quest is not to care.
Underwater prisms influence my paranoia until dissecting my brain becomes my obsession.
Washington Irving and you drink at a sailor's bar in a Confederate cemetery for misfits.
I search for your shadow, but dreams of others in impossible pain are only what come to mind.
Shifting from the elements on shore, David Hume waves to us as Christian bigots choose virgins.

I translate the conversation that lake-effect snow has with the crew of the SS Edmund Fitzgerald.
Idiosyncrasies allow caged lions to imagine the taste of their masters when their tongues swell.
Knowing that the whole is greater than the sum of its parts, the archbishop enters you from behind.
Blackened eyes in Switzerland are very rare as philosophers laugh and create money from free will.
You do not know what voyage I have embarked on. My mind is liquid; plus, you cannot tell time.
Our passion for adversity is renewed as we push forward continually. We are reminded that killing is our goal.

With calculated intentions, you call my name. You have survived, yet the echo is absent.
Unlike literature, I am mad and in a place where only those who are forgotten think to be called human.
We contemplate the reflective obsession where tides possess a much deeper persuasive quality.
And you are a character too fragile to convey pain, the one who is sincerely loved yet pitied.
This is our life at sea. We are surrounded by death on our way to destroy for those who abhor choices.
We will become legendary heroes respected for the ruthless way by which we have extinguished other souls.

Venus called me again and asked for information about the possessions found by her ubiquitous descendants.
That is when the switchblade struck my heart and the glowing coals illuminated sin at night.
As I beg for forgiveness, you prod me every time I speak about self-sacrifice and adversity.
Mariners in love with things hidden recognize that all flesh under goodness is just camouflage.
Angels wearing homicide bustiers note that those who believe are more distressed than those who are lost.
Cold, strange, and uninhibited, the critic gods assure me that the rarest talent is no talent to lose.

At midnight, tanned legs curl around my neck, dismissing all my thoughts and focusing my desire.

Maurice Chevalier in the galley mixes cocaine with manuka honey to produce a lasting forever.

Brahms' symphonic themes lull whales into watching ambiguous images and recalling their ancestral enemies.

One's antisocial behavior aboard the ship brings out the whips to record the damage done by having selfish faith.

The wisdom of muted silence celebrates music Mozart never wrote.

Being truthful, we rehabilitate each other's longing to be nude, insane, and in love without remorse.

Letting go is difficult when I watch you atop me glistening, with insight of flames devouring us.

As the sirens linger, what seemed exquisitely dangerous now appears to be no more than graceless mental bleeding.

Ascribing to us questionable accomplishments, Augustine kicks the near dead overboard.

Polaroid mistresses survived, for optimistic declensions come with arms to conquer the opposition.

Knowing I'm going to die, I praise myself and hallucinate about fearing no human-made god.

I admire your buttocks: calculus in splendor. I am the fool fixated on my inner murderer.

Part III: The Earth Cries

Foraging in biblical texts, I find the overlooked centerfolds of naked maidens in blessed waters.

Thinking philosophically, we are on your backs in front of mirrors reliving our mistakes.

Liberty leads the people while I erase sailors from contextual fulfillment, because I alone am me.

Van Eyck, unfamiliar with the grotesque, provokes qualms about obliterated inner structures.

Without any forlorn letters, Mary places her knee on my shoulder and tosses away her wedding ring.

Unaware that the next century has arrived, I explain justified humanism to an anxious Louise Labé.

At a wet bar before I go drinking, Hopper asks if he can paint my imaginary lifestyle.

In a skimpy red dress without panties, you understand that your prospects are based on my ideas.

Depressed anarchists in drag for the sake of mobility lean on me for advice about mass suicide.

I kiss all the naked young women on their backs and between their legs, ignoring all the messiahs.

Awesome in conception, self-fashioned actors plead the case for words to replace rash actions.

The ship without wind struggles in settings known only to painters with palettes of modern pastels.

Undistinguishable colors lead Frankenstein's monster to the mirror, where he sees only my face.

In heaven, history is a place mat for the energies invested in knowing every outcome after the fact.

Punching at the combined forces, I find an expedient way to exterminate my thoughts of revenge.

You can't explain what I am thinking, only what I feel when the blood drains from my wounds.

The ship commandeers a schooner. The female crew is captured. Their wombs are sewed to save humankind.

Watching dogs, I ask God how much philosophical reflection comes with barking declarations.

Russian centurions and Taliban ragmen fight to see who will perform the nastiest tragic acts.

Raping the voluptuous Sabine women, I advocate for classical antiquity as the shadow of Brutus looms.

Barabbas in community theater tells us all that we possess meaning only if death is our beginning.

I still do not understand James Joyce. He seems to be a series of centerpieces missing a masterpiece.

Naked with insignificance, I find it impossible to explain my pairing of personality and perpetual failure.

"You hate me," you whisper, pulling out the blade you just stabbed me with and licking the blood excitedly.

Nameless slaves are sold at churches so faithless nuns can hide the truth under their religious veneration.

Finally, with Chatterley and Bovary enjoying drugs and champagne, I accept the person I could have been.

Courbet asks if the forest floor is mere camouflage for the footsteps long hidden after amorous encounters.

Shakespeare, drinking aquavit with Emerson, sighs as he undresses Monroe to test her reasoning.

This would be to my liking if the seas were not full of poisonous reasons proving that the mind deceives.

Reinventing myself after Gettysburg, I usher at Ford's Theater to show God's influence over humankind.

I cannot get back to the place where I thought I had my first thoughts, my mind now knowing itself.

Dead ends continue to build up until what was once an answer is now but another question.

Saboteurs force dream chasers to digest American morals, which are absent of life and transformative energy.

On the outskirts of the last moment, negations take on force and close down all valued opposites.

Uninterrupted, we agree with Socrates, because his context switches to incoherence when heard.

Dismal and on the hunt for mermaids, we compete for irreverence so that nobody is harmed.

Abstract oil on canvas is the essential design for Neoplatonist thinking between thoughts.

Behind hidden recognitions, Beethoven strips Cinderella and places a slipper on Sleeping Beauty.

Discharged from the war, I elaborate on theology, only to be thought of as an iconoclastic romantic.

Tacitus in red velvet asks why those lost in love never remember they have been already forgotten.

Coherent angels with a branding iron to my brain look for reasons why love fades when it is consumed.

Examining a wastebasket, you accept the condemning of the peasants but not the blessing of the poor.

Parallel galaxies in multidimensional universes crack the code as forever blocks views of infinity.

Back in my cabin, the sun bewilders nature's charm. You materialize as sand in my hourglass.

My astrocytes are bewildered, but they uninhibitedly and lucidly receive spiritual accolades and divine transcendence.

Boating on the Seine, Lucifer and I visit brothels near the gates of heaven, hoping to have the ideal.

Unfolding in senseless corridors, intellectuals begin to seek the hereafter even though they are here within.

Summer is gone. Voluntary restrictions now exemplify the ocean's rage in the face of catastrophic holism.

I cannot wait to hold you now that my face has been mutilated and only my dreams remain.
Wealthy gods with little faith in closed-minded humankind seek refuge in Freud's writings.
You, desperate with my clawing against the earth's turmoil choose to harangue every exit.
While we are suspended in a sexual act, a solo violin reveals what inspires sacrileges fables.
Stray fingers in a menage a trois use probing to complement every achievement that erupts from blossoming.
Accolades after sentiment, duel with the absurdity of breasts being sanctified before suckled.

Beset by hazards, we attack those unsullied by integrity, catching them in our nets.
Claudius, unaware of the circumstances of his death, looks to hell for identifying absurdity.
In the confrontation, all those who opposed thought by thinking, lingered in line to have you.
On deck, one voice shouts, "I believe in love." Merciful Judas hangs him from the highest mast.
Intimidating jealousy forbids assassination of those found voguish in defining sexual dreams.
Your courtesan's conscience is bruised by the last customer to lick what is left of your indulgent pride.

Monet unleashed in contradiction points to Donizetti to make the latter aware of the psyche in the future.
After removing the stake from my heart, I toss it onto the fire, where my body lies under dying dolphins.
From life, I move to art, my melancholy sinking with crystal images laden with the unforeseen.
Judging me insane, heaven condemns me to fish for men in places where only the surreal exists.
With an ultimately invaluable idea, I continue forward until a soldier nails me adjacent to Spartacus.
In quarrels about the time being, I turn to the past, when my tongue was coated with crimson irony.

Assaulted by enigma turncoats, I comprehend you as being between opposite ends of credibility.
Theologists preaching inner strife remain after the gold-model hypocrisy contradicts absurdity.
Vanquished by Milton, Dryden repeats the call for innocence to be subjugated by unrequited love.
Then you and I become impossible to comprehend without our tears that are caused by an improbable question.
Music starts to spurt from the earth's genitals. We all know we are possessed to believe nothing.
Counting on uncertain treasure, the ship leaves modern realms to find what endlessly torments us.

On course to find wishes in dreams, we destroy all life that is concealed beneath the mocking resentment.

Plagiarist doctrines openly admit that morality confines the soul to those who can promote extinction.

I, on the other hand, am beyond what is essentially insane. I'm developing constructs that are far from acceptance.

Quantum physics marries Electra on the same ground where we curtailed the meanderings of Jesus.

Thunder continues to light reason where all the Buddhists proclaim those of the East to be masters of slavery.

Traveling through destruction, I understand that words are impotent to convince us to trust.

Becoming religious perfection, Heidegger insists that we question choice instead of chance.

Caressing your swollen thighs under the empirical light, I listen to you repeat my lies.

Trading me for the Queen of Diamonds before Porta's analysis reminded the pariahs of both fantasy and reality.

Cousins back from the Machiavellian wars grasp from antiquity to tomorrow every blood relative sacrificed.

What the terms foresaw, I forgot as you emerged from platitudes created by philosophers.

I know that pain explores all avenues humankind can invent, so, with thorns of plenty, I rub my eyes.

Sicilian monsters emerge once Huginn and Muginn join with Darwin to study cocoa leaves.

Tears will come anyway as the sailors in black face are danced to the firing squad.

Amusing ladders made of vibrations seek better definitions when the truth is spoken.

I kick a head down the path, while my eyes behold what mirrors never wanted me to see.

Then, as the smoke clears, I see that there is only a bugler burying the remains of the dead-minded.

I never existed, so I cannot be found—because I have been negotiating my punishment.

The Three Graces, working the circuit, wait for the return of the Four Horsemen.

Spreading the cheeks of all my lovers, I make up my mind to explain my senses.

Though you make me feel very special, I despise the loss of my migraine disturbances.

Fluids leak from organisms on sheets. Catechism characters watch saints disrobe.

Now I have a chance to speak my mind to those who believe that immortality is found in words.

After the journey, I rest my mind on the souls of my ancestors who believed in existentialism.

Penelope and my daughter recognize me as I walk from my flesh into fame and misfortune.

The trip took place like most, on the curvature of my brown eyes and without any disillusionment.

Alive but dead, I embrace all the knowledge that promotes the idea that life can never be sent to death.

In your embrace forever, I have not been gone. Rather, I've been prevented from beginning.

Ulysses, Achilles, Paris, and Helen have become a globe. With it, we cherish our forgetfulness.

With a sword in my hand and a gun in my pocket, I am the last one to surrender my thoughts.

Connecting my allegorical aspirations, I and me stop to ask for illusory, exploratory directions.

Mesmerized by "I am," I decide to debate my character while I imagine him.

Now very insane, I need to stretch from dreams and move into pure science to realize where I have been.

Those faraway, sculptured figures are just my id gone farther from thought, from all justification.

Undressing every woman I know, I ask what pleasures are provided with the memories I have made.

God evolves, and I am endlessly absent from whom I will never want to become—again and again.

Artwork, "Al este lado" by Spanish artist Alex Alemany – e-mail: alex@alexalemany.com – www.alexalemany.com

Book *Three*

INTELLIGENCE GREETS INSANITY AS THEY BOTH DISAPPEAR

ELEMENTS

Improbable,
The loneliness
My heart feels,
Even though I know
I am lost.
Words
Diminish
The acts.
Archetypes
In art and drama
Claim lives.
Chained to columns
Without assumptions,
And be it sky
Or sea,
An enemy
Contradicts time
By challenging
Thought.
The elements
Know
They are without
Rules,
And the gods
Regularly
Gamble with the elements.
I regret
I lost my invitation

Photograph by Scottish photographer Stuart McAllister

To see beyond
Fate,
Because
The consequence
Is confronting
A mirror
That
Knows
My soul
And how
To administer pain.
In this reflection, I see
Questions,
Questions.

DUTHIE: JUST A STREET IN A WATERFRONT TOWN

He spent the night with her.
When he woke up,
The night
Was no longer in his eyes.
His best friend's wife
Lay beside him as he reflected on
Cherie amour.

He spent the night with her.
When he woke up,
The night
Was no longer in his eyes.
His best friend's friend
Lay beside him.
Southern belle reflections.

He spent the night with her.
When he woke up,
The night
Was no longer in his eyes.
His best girl had slit her wrists.
He lay beside her.
Frenzied flame reflections.

He spent the night with her.
When he woke up,
The night
Was no longer in his eyes.
His best girl was dead.
He lay beside himself.
Nameless angel reflections.

She spent the night alone.
When she woke up,
The night
Was no longer in her eyes
Her lover had lied.
He lay beside his best friend's wife.
Clear light reflections.

Artwork by Spanish artist Modesto Roldan

Marlowe, Marlow, and Marlowe

Being touched inside like a flame twice afire,
    I ran from the allusions of forbidden novels
Into the arms of intuition. I knew not my faults
    Then the wisdom of the future, sung by naked angels in rhapsody, touched me
Saints and I embraced, our chrysalis shed, our toil and bloodlines behind us
    Amid an absence of sanity and commitment divided by absurdity
Now I search for the remedies that will unite the past without comprehension
    My feelings gone astray in decimal points, counting circular admissions to infinity
The wandering of desire melts as I wade toward the underside of reality;
    God yawns in the distance; God always yawns when my name is mentioned

I become the difference between who I am and me - the simple and invariable genius
    With the world in turmoil, my mind enfolds as your love defines difficulty and detachment
I strip you and smell the aromas of comfortable past entrances where sins were erased
    Melancholy memories on barstools reflect the delusion in colored bottles
Too many sacrifices to understand that sacrifices were always called moral behavior.
    Restless from our liberation from conformity, I lick the sweat from your breasts,
Dreaming of her dreaming of me dreaming of us in a dream knowing it is yet to be dreamt
    Exceptions more than expectations are needless when legs are open to audiences
At the trial, I am found guilty of loving without caring whether my life has meaning
    Wives with scars from retelling lies recall rough sex without other aspects of awareness.

A cigarette burns toward my psychological inclinations toward a consummate suicide
    I enter from the back door and reveries from deep fantasy cloud the dagger at your throat
Bipolar in a puppy's cage, I hear eagles swoop down on drunken doves tearing off their corsets
    "Forgive me," I hear the inmates cry as the whips wrap around our necks in detached stories
Separating fear from action, I believe the armistice means freedom - but death is all that surrounds me
    Acerbic intellectuals cry for Dorothy Parker and give me morphine to comfort my thoughts
We slice through the bitten beginnings to find the end, but bittersweet coils are all that remain
    Maiden's sick from repellants masturbate in the minds of young men who will die soon
Since the lobotomy, I excel at parallel enthusiasm for still-life nudes bathed in my blood
    Squeezing my eyelids shut, I smell your multiple lovers queuing up to reappear.

The encore - liquor-filled illusions of juniper strippers rehearsing for invisible portraits

   At sea in winter with nothing but you tattooed on my biceps, I wait for prophecies

Knowing torture is the equivalent of sweet violins that underestimate my love for you

   I am dreaming I fall asleep - which changes the journey in my nightmares

I watch you hammer nails through my heart as crucifixes drip blood from my thoughts

   The enemies pass, whine, and reflect on the enigma of ambiguity of death from sorrows

I know you climaxed on my bed with your lovers' assassins who appall claustrophobic regretfulness

   Against the grain, against the turmoil, against the odds, time poisons your imagination

With you, without me, outclassed in the thoughts of dead symbolists I lose my artistic awareness.

   It is now that the tears of surrealism mount metaphysical abstractions inside me

Diamond-shaped crystals grind my irises out of the whiteness for whores to see my pain

   Becoming the striking, paranoid self-portrait behind the mirror chained to tattered caresses

Now with your body on my back, I taste this expectant specter in discourse with spirits

   A prism, like women bathed in infinite beauty, drips into shadows of things I have left undone

Serving the last bacchanals, I become what I was before I became what I could never be

   The heel of your foot pressing against my teeth watches meaning disappear from words

Somewhere from the grave, I see daylight while philosophers contemplate my absence

   The explosions where breasts expand into countless distractions taunt my desires for you

You laughed when your lover went down on your boyfriend just to sample a taste of me

   In the interim, I slit my wrists, dancing in circles while joyous blood splashes the walls.

Hearing the church bells outside, imprisoned by maturity I lovingly die in Hera's arms

   I met the inmates inside the puzzle, trying to relocate characters lost in liberation novels

They and I with them, and I without me, are on the outside, looking at defiant illusions emerging

   I reviled my appetite more than did the others who weep for the sins of menstruating women,

I forever crave that smell of feminine power that wafts from the damp ringlets between your legs

   Restless accusers scorn me for ejaculating between the split tongue of war and fortune

Laughing at sanity, Achilles curls his hands around my neck, pressing cut glass into my lips

   There are those, not me, who say irrational tyrants cannot measure mindless compassion

The wind has no enemies; it just gathers my intended words and mixes them with arrogance

   Relentless in my search for what comes with wanting all that is without is remembrance.

I continue the journey down the paths of confusion and madness, sailing on this somber sea
   The sane have no quarrel with those who defile baptism in search of completeness
Without any boundaries, all the liquids assemble and extinguish any hope for my love
   We pull oars. We are whipped. We rape each other's thoughts before we expire
Then the waves decide to kiss the shores. Some find comfort in nevermore,
   But not us; the sinners who wear multiple crowns of thorns
Not you; a perpetual reflection liquidly peripheral in ethereal gothic images
   And not me; this discarded vagrant adventurer waiting to bite your nipples again
Count the days but not with numbers, paint them the color of death resurrecting defeat
   Cultures and time will be the only harm that comes to those who extinguish believing.

   Days later—not yet now, but far from then—
At their office, I sit in a comfortable leather chair with my mind unraveling a myth
   I wait for the poet, the narrator, and the detective.

Artwork by French artist Audrey Marienkoff

MORE THAN YOU THOUGHT

The police arrived.
I showed them your lifeless body.
Your mouth had been cut out,
The part I hated the most,
A mouth that often sneered,
But with lips very full and soft.

I handed the police your heart.
It was not heart-shaped at all.
There were bullet holes and stab wounds.
They asked you about me
You were unimpressed and swaggering
Who knows where hindsight leads us.

The revolver was still in my hands;
A bloody electric knife, on the table;
Champagne, in Waterford crystal.
The winds at Penistone Crags were howling.
The escalator stuttered in my mind.
Blue police became white doctors.

No one was dead except for me.
I was dead to the world, as it seemed to be.
Kafka was sitting and reading
About Cupid and lobotomies.
In the next room, I turned to myself.
I was busy punishing myself.

Photograph of French Model/Artist She nandoah

The doctors were premonitions
Of the fall that forever always takes.
I cut my arms and saw you waving.
Uncomfortable in a ghostly performance,
You closed your hands around my throat,
Our memories from Gaslight spilling.

Then the moon decided to pray.
Figurines and cut glass displayed battered badges.
Those without examples covered their faces.
I was in pantomime as a paranoid schizophrenic.
Braque put us all in tarot-colored cubes.
Only death saved us once the beginning began again.

I watched myself in shape but not in form, contradictory in meaning.
Rafael painted your breasts on the Madonna of lost souls.
I was aboard the Flying Dutchman. My ideas tangled with your rage.
You, yet to perform, became an abridged transition to savage enthusiasm.
You recalled having visions of God lecturing you about anthropomorphic reality.
Still, it was 1929 in Spain. I dined with Dali and Gala while bulls charged.

Lyricism was too brash for the functionally elite to keep beneath their bloodstained sins.
With my hatchet, I attacked the meaningless nonsense with annotations.
The laughter was harsh when our sixties' sexuality surpassed wildlife eroticism.
Giacometti handed me a drink, saying his premonitions were always my illusions.
Lost in forgotten territory, I demanded that my hearing be released from blindness.
Ladders arrived to take the insane back to the sculptures that created them.

The rooks are the odds markers, the legends to all wars and geometric games.
Eventually, my negative realism became an altered version of Pygmalion's simplicity.
Bourbon-striped beds swirled lunacy among the innocent whose eyes lacked observation.
Elastic Freudian-Roman dancers exchanged imaginative fragments of their egos.
I welcomed the threshold and made love to all the sources that exposed artistry.
Alchemists floated dream images over Magritte as he played a Ma piece on the cello.

Singing, "You will never leave. Please never let me go, never let me go to Katmandu,"

The hangman pushed forward. Mother Teresa handed me a sweet lei from Maui.
Who will be my music, tell my story, and seed the firmament for idolatrized settings?
Railroad spikes go "bang, bang," the gelatin percussion crashing inside my head.
Dada rococoists inflame the inconsequential illusionists by making obsessions legal.
The rewarded postimpressionists lament my art-nouveau consciousness.

Counting the errors in my thoughts, I am disguised as the firebird from Bethlehem
All white, the pure white, the white surrealism designed for Gudrun and Strindberg.
Now, with hallucinatory acid poured down my throat, I preclude my absence.
Sarcastic nightmarish forms become undressing women hiding inside themselves.
Breaking apart lemon-drop gradations, I draw André Breton nursed in a shallow space.
Flying through windows, suiters despoil Ulysses' estate, frolic while ellipses develop.

Thinking inside my bloodline, Italians slumber uneasily amid my continuance.
Velázquez laments that he is a modern painter who rejects all meaning without fantasy.
As for me, I have returned from Tenth Street, where I kissed the statue of St. Anthony.
Carolina Moon and Dusty in Memphis cannot orchestrate the temporal-lobe blues.
I know long ago has no circumference to entice. I am just a physical sarcophagus.
Twilight indifferences, in dynamic incoherence, drip into God's imagination silently.

When I am in this mood, insanity locks onto a sexual eternity suspended in antiquity
Paraphrasing the legitimate, I offer my scarred arm as a hand to Klimt, which he cuts
Against my will, tropical poets sniff at my lips, which kiss every ivory-breasted woman.
I realize I am forever a stranger to myself. Hybrid surrealists burn my work in praise.
Wagner, never in sync with expectation, plays heavily with orgasmic reverie at my grave.
Enigmas inhale the ambiguities as I cascade back to the sea to listen for intervention.

When the police arrived,
Your naked fresco annoyed them.
A woman and a child fingered the cracks in our future.
You pushed an ice pick into my awareness.
An ocean of psychological impediments
Took my place. I was no longer me.

Photograph by Canadian photographer Bonita (Bonnie) Harris

Mary Magdalene Makes a Suspicious Collect Call

Act I: The Characters and Their Motives

We four knew
    Excellence by profession. We had been
Angered since the ramblings of Freud.
    Down at the riverfront bars
Fighting drunken sailors,
    The lowest-level prostitutes
Interrupted our conversation.
    How do we overthrow complacency?
Drinks are served:
    Beers and rum.
The server shows her breasts:
    Insufferably white with ruby-red nipples.
Jack takes his dagger out.
    Hyde grins.
Dorian calls the server over.
    For a scant few pennies, she is under the table.
The sucking sounds and the visible act
    Bring on cheers.
A circle finds its way to us.
    I hate this century and the last.
I yearn for weapons that kill quickly, that
    Never miss, that leaves one remorseless.
A stargazer approaches while I am washing my hands.
    He wants to sell me nude photos of infants.
I point to the window.
    Outside, I slit his throat—twice—because I can.
Back at the table, I order more bottles of dark rum.
    Hyde smiles and says, "Time to terrorize. I hate this scum."
I hear Gilbert and Sullivan in the background,

A mix of supremacy and gutter ramblings.
Jack calls us to the bar.
We need to stretch our comprehension.
Our willingness to be bold adventurers
Undeterred by blood seeping from every cut.
Selecting the works of Man Ray, we dab our darts in poison.
Jake Barnes makes the first hit, though he is behind his shadow.
Missing the North Star, Brutus stumbles before emerging.
Weldon Penderton's lips are pursed as he endures closeted remorse.
I take aim at Emma Bovary, the literary equivalent of my desires.
We four remain frustrated while waiting for Frankenstein, the man of pieces.
Cleaning colors from Emma's delinquent innocence, Hyde questions a prostitute.
She removes her dress, which is when we find that she is also he.
Jack is fascinated, looking forward to acts of unbelievably savage brutality.
Two child whores, thinking we are approachable, come forward.
I toss coins and they follow, they follow,
Expecting more, expecting more, more—always more.
That is when Dorian, fixing his cravat, speaks: "They all want more."
There should be a punishment for more and a bigger punishment forever more.
Jack viciously turns on his companion and slices her/his face.
He stabs at it, slices it, punctures it, tears at it, cuts it feverishly.
We clap and add our personal trademarks to the wretched victim.
Hyde rapes the children and leaves them with nightmarish visions of paradise.
With his bejeweled nightstick, Dorian beats to death a drunken couple.
Feeling profoundly free, I shout, "Start the revolution," as I drink whiskey from my flask.
An Englishman mentions that life is only for those who can survive.
Are we interested? Are we ruthless enough? Yes, we are!

We meander through the night, goading Jack to murder indiscriminately.
Hyde, bipolar, is sometimes shaken and sometimes repulsed. Killing is a whim.
Dorian will never be humbled, so the suffering before death is important.
Icarus flew too close to the sun. We singe the innocent who are distant from god.
We are transformative artists changing life into meaningful flesh art.
Discarded victims high on forecast ideology kiss the rings of religious egotists.
We kill them slowly, watching their faces turn from spotty to gray.
Acquainted with disgust, we walk into a cockroach-ridden room where lovers tangle.

The blood splashes over all the walls as two dead bodies become one.

Dorian uses an axe on half-waking victims, asking them to spread their legs.

Mary Shelley's forlorn creation is always on our mind and never arrives.

Dawn: the disagreeable time when Jesus meets us and we embrace until we meet again.

A Short Break to Contemplate

I hate the daylight,
The brightness,
The flowers opening,
The children off to school,
The baby buggies being pushed.
I hate all that is nourished in the sunshine.
My destiny is to eliminate accomplishment,
Playgrounds, and women on the streets, pretend
Waifs, and beginners asking for spare change.
Nighttime is required for me to proceed—
The darkness,
The moonless nights when fools die and whores sing,
Sharpening knives, cleaning guns, and singing "Amazing Grace."
Pure hatred is the last true emotion.
Death to those deserving.
Humanity needs a culling crew.
Jack, Hyde, Dorian, and I volunteered.
God commands us. He was drunk in those days, the Bible recounts.
He was under a beautiful, blue-eyed, big-breasted, blonde-haired Nordic woman.
God never felt more alive. Thor had sent her as a gift.
God loved to watch her strip. He loved those breasts.
He gorged himself on those pert, pink nipples.
At the gate, the minorities protested the woman's whiteness.
A man with underworld connections approached God.
Cards were passed and money was exchanged. A few Jews were hired to write a story.
Clouds cleared. All the Greek gods arrived.
Nude Roman goddesses dressed as cheerleaders strut in the garden.
Virgil and Homer eagerly invent psychoanalysis.
While overhearing Aphrodite scolding Hermes,

God reads the script with a grin. "I never rest!"
He hollers for Michelangelo,
 Who asks about genius?
The promoters state, "Doubt far exceeds intelligence."
 A symphony begins, Mozart, I believe.
Zeus comments, "Let people run into each other with daggers."
 Bacchus giggles before saying, "They seem very willing to die."
A loud trumpet sounds.
 The games have begun.
Jack, Hyde, Dorian, and I escape into literature.
 That is the last time we are together.
However, our legends linger.
 We evaporate into thought inhaled by millennia.

Act II: Incorporating Thought

"It is all about timing," said the wolf to the rabbit on a spit. See how the world revolves?
 Judas, wearing a dress and high heels, asks me if I want to earn some silver.
I open his skull. He runs, watching his organs being devoured by his thoughts.
 The celebration continues with blinding snow and hot tubs filled with scorpions.
Parallel boredom tracks lead me to find the depths of my sight when my eyes are closed.
 Banging on the outskirts of poetical libel, my shame is calmed by my absence.
Hearing rumbling from the next epoch, I raise my sword to fight indifference.
 Not the show I intended. Searing flames toast my heart and dissolve my soul.
Women milk themselves as umbrella tips are inserted into their nostrils along with cocaine.
 On my own, I scour the entrails handed out by sawdust entrepreneurs.
Providing input for contemplation, I reenter my dreams and run through the nightmares.
 Challenging my existence, I untie razor wire before placing it around my neck.
The echo of her good-bye tiptoes inside my head, finds the edges, and marches back.
 Without recourse, the night darkens from a dull glassy color to stillbirth blue.
All the connections become mad; the neurons, unable to find grounding, exit into psychosis.
 The swans flying between the subjects are unbothered by streaming judgements.
Lethal, tremulous blurs linger forever. Contrasting sight lags behind curious illusions.
 In innocence, it is hard to accept the escaping mementos becoming blood avenues.
Exhilarating self-destiny only unfolds to those who have a yearning to devour eternity.

Ovid, Plutarch, and Plato find Lautrec. The four
Appear on Ed Sullivan as the Beatles.
   Nature is quartered and sold.
Pathetic religions and stories abound.
   Counterfeit obsessions take hold.
Examined lives turn to commerce.
   Ships of destruction gather momentum.
Death practices are performed on the innocent.
   Indigenous tributaries dry up and disappear.
Paralysis, carved into human shapes, takes charge.
   God's contention appraises itself.
Whirling insistence creates glory from gold.
   Gilded swords drip blood as Hamlet sighs.
Moody, melancholy cold and exhilaration.
   The statue of Mary—all the glory.
Historians pledged to stain analogical thinking.
   Nothing lasts for long but momentum.
Deciphered, we asked ourselves who should hang first.
   Landmarks are advertisements for the triumphant beast.
Passion on exhibit, drinks served, women raped, and arms scarred.
   Age shirking. Love founded on false conceptions.
Metaphors now hide from racists who cannot pronounce destiny.
   Bullets are fired, hitting impressions without leaving a trace.
Beautiful Lauren makes cupcakes, showing there is time for love and sanity.
   I am forever speaking to myself about misconceptions about my being.
The ambulance has arrived. I hear the Spanish accents of those dressed in hospital white and
then I see the straitjacket.
   The police need to search and steal.
I am found with myself, playing cards with the person I call me.
   The opera begins. Is it Verdi or Puccini?
I receive a call from San Francisco. It is Toasty, leaving for Honolulu.
   In The Canterbury Tales, the minor characters leave to join Beowulf.
They meet up with Henry Fleming to pillage hospitals and funeral homes.
   Only the lonely live without confirmation of life.

Transferred by the ones in blue uniforms, I become an acquiescent patient.

Outsiders weep, protesting my institutionalization.

Screamers attest to the massacre and retrieve importance for destiny.

I leave my head behind. The workers use it for shaping rumors.

Who can forgive the essence for being more than the intention?

Fathers Merrin and Karris are questioned downtown.

Only Merrin has the correct solution. Karris, acting psychotically, is crucified.

There are no furtive interiors left in me. Love creates holes where passion leaks.

Baker dances, thinking about the Second Coming. Henriette Grindat sculpts thighs in my mind.

Joni Mitchell plays steel drums, sending coded messages to my Greenpeace crew.

I remember Jack, who loved killing and ripping open human flesh;

Hyde, never quite mentally right and needing to see how much pain could be endured;

Dapper Dorian, knowing that those who died by his hand were grateful for his mercy.

Intensive geniuses distinct for their senseless preoccupation now live in memory

Tarantella hieroglyphs are found in castles made of sand reminding us all art rescues.

Intermission. Drinks are served. Eye those whom you resent.

Act IV: Covering Up Our Nakedness

I stopped where the postman rings twice. It is an asylum for people who borrow accomplishments.

John Garfield is hopelessly in love—the dance, the bewilderment.

She stands there—Lana Turner. Lana Turner. I give my best James Dean impression.

Scrambled intonations rarely result in any transformative landscapes.

Warring epithets underwrite those who deserve only misery and receive all of it.

No longer under the shadow of my friends, I feel the need to self-mutilate.

The Devil decorated his views on misfits and apostolic nuance. Hatred sustains success.

In the varicose views, I perceive elements of transposition beyond recovery.

I watch your mouth condemn our time, yet I live with continual sexual fantasies.

Your excuses, my significance—skimming emotions across mindless persistence.

Soon, another murder will be committed amid massive bells ringing for the faithful.

The enchantment is surreal, and what is bizarre transcends what is not.

Lights out. Oh, a beginning. Dig your heels in, you with gloves spiked with death talons.

Oh, love is here. Please, one question: when do you intend on killing me?

Porfiry Petrovich announces the brazen differences between psychological treatments
All the incendiary writers giggle as Lincoln leaves for the theater.

Inaccurate expressions leading to different historical versions tell me to percieve
Those thought characters invented by outcasts live indefinitely in our minds.

Calendar-imagined dolls surrender from wax, reassembling amid a rude awakening.
Clever lighting allows those with a thousand possibilities to hide their enigmas.

Tender beds await the country girl's spirituality without contempt on her menstrual days.
I await the seamstress, the amateur who knows how to lie with a smile.

My enormous intelligence drowns in sins built on frozen impudence.
We are what we choose to be. She is a dream who needs my wings to enfold her.

In my enthusiasm for belligerence, I claim there is an exorcist who is the next leader of an epoch.
Jung tells me all weather storms shall awaken from preexistence.

Finding my lips in a chalice with my lover's vagina, I contemplate forever—forever.
Knowing I am going to die by my own hand allows my condemning of splattered canvases.

Tangible compassion is for those suffering from expanded paranoia.
Your footsteps recover in my mind after I make my feeble attempts at suicide.

Now the paradoxical cheer for my intellect ignited from electrodes in my brain.
Voluntary hallucinations inhabit the torn canvas that Dali left for Delvaux.

Athos, Porthos, Aramis, and I listen to modern jazz,
The boundaries past Mozart, past Beethoven, and past classical.

The combed independence slickening the before.
Poisoned minnows are swallowed for astonishment.

We ponder why we should not murder every human on earth with our own hands.
Jam sessions with heretics and characters from Watership Down

Have learned very well from Jack how to hate
Hyde taught me to feel envy from the deepest part of my soul.

Dorian said that obsessive confidence was crucial for killing.
In a jazz joint on the docks, three women are drugged with passion to sing The Odyssey.

I know them: Penelope, Circe, and Calypso. I have had them. They realized my fantasy.
There is no out, only a crawl space between knowing and accomplishing.

Gendarmes, return me back to the beginning, where Homer is thinking.
Ulysses, promoting Mediterranean easy listening, tells me not to waste time.

Selfishly, I lure a dirtied-face Asian girl outside and gleefully slit her throat.
The sax is stretching, about to reach its peak, but never getting there.

The drums, tumbling, keep a cadence. I am very free and mad.

Photos of John Coltrane and Lester Young fall from the grimy walls.

If only I had a machine gun for a clean sweep of this derelict humanity.

The music hits a crescendo. I wrap a towel around a Negro's neck and twist it.

The crowd, drunk from masturbating against corn-fed cows, enters the tomb.

I leave the bar with a misshapen young waitress wearing silver braces.

The midnight sun or moon sparkles in her eyes. I am again Meursault.

We dance to Elvis in a dive where beggars steal hearts from angels.

Six sailors, high on paint thinner, approach me with money for her.

I watch them take her outside and rape her continually.

Then I shoot them—each one—and watch rats assemble and suck their blood.

Deliverance now is a harpoon hurled by Hercules that grabs my attention.

I roam the streets and kill Dickens characters, their destinies incomplete.

In my apartment, mad Russians play psycho. Stravinsky makes overtures.

Their need is for copulating with Nijinsky while playing roulette with a sword.

Blonde Nordic serpents with massive breasts rehearse as Wagner fondles Hitler.

It is easy to see the distance. Time elevates, needing to level out its circumference.

Lipstick transvestites on their elbows sing arias from Madame Butterfly.

I rotate the chambers of my only love: a silver Smith and Wesson.

My imprecations, now ripe, are gangrenous with my fearful love.

Liquor is served and drugs are passed while revolutionary language is expressed.

The knights with spears through their armor foretell of unapproachable inspirations.

Down in the subway, I sample the brain of Narcissus, hoping to explain my insane sanity.

Delightful absinthe fries my thoughts of a painting in Arles, one dreamt by Van Gogh.

I am just listening to the distinct sound of irrationality inflated by bohemian chance.

The voyage being widened, I need to select my female prey,

Those few milky-white-freckled receptacles without a future.

Drinking cognac, I wipe my blade with virgin blood, grinning with anaconda revenge.

Piano keys—Art Tatum or Chopin. My mind is claimed by absurdist solo requests.

Horns announce my presence, Dante takes my top hat and coat.

The flames singe those who are spiritually accomplished, their spirits always aglow.

Can you hear them, those Brandywine beatnik intellectual poets shaping innovations?

"Mr. Ginsberg. Dorothy Parker. Please?" the Kerouac announcer asks.

The Black Panthers, dressed as American storm troopers, take the stage.

According to the manifesto, I am to be revered, electrocuted, and mummified.

Caucasians frightened by baptism place bets on runner-up saints.

Pavarotti is swinging with a Brazilian whore who is high on ecstasy.

Post-Kantian philosophers give up hope and start shooting heroin.

Gatsby arrives and wants to discuss murder. Jack asks, "May I buy you a daisy?"

I ask him if a lark is ascending or if Rommel has left for the African front.

He wants respect because he was in a war, but he could not remember if he is alive.

Hyde states that once conceit's eclipse crosses the ocean, we will kill indiscriminately.

Gatsby, now in love with Madame Bovary, experiments with sex toys.

Someone tells me about a place without regret. I point to a drugstore.

Once the bombs begin to fall, Frenchmen smoke cigarettes as Edith sings.

D. H. Lawrence heads out West to fail once more at raising consciousness.

With a banjo on my knee, I carry painkillers across the borderline.

Nothing is contemplated when torture accompanies the spasms from exotic orgasms.

I walk on with my mind in one hand and the reality of knowing in the other.

The smoothness permeates the depth of every question I consider.

Moses in a tie-dyed robe collects a five-dollar cover at the door.

He is arguing with David about parking spaces and money issues.

Ancient bravado signals the night's peak. Is Paris burning?

Nude with Collette, my love mimes Macbeth.

The doors open. I spend six shells and then reload with my black thoughts.

Dizzy follows with a night in Tunisia. Why am I without you?

Cold rationalism, one step beyond common thought, is next on the agenda.

Nazi trucks and Wall Street tycoons erase constitutional rights.

The night continues, Picasso giving lectures on promiscuity.

The loudspeaker announces Mike Bloomfield.

The slave culture and dead Christian transcendence measure our steps to the white drinking fountains.

Then the bullets fly. Garbo takes the stage.

The cameras accent her ethnicity. She sings without a voice.

Lenin and I conceal nothing and advocate for supremely quick deaths.

Trumpets adhere to a higher power. I take the stage to grand applause.

The interview is relevant. "Comprehend or die," I shout.

I liken this elasticity to caramelized thought in an incandescent precept made holy.

Concerned with historical sufficiency, Hart Crane beds down with Jack London.

Taylor dumping Burton consigns the word husband to a dissatisfactory sanity clause.

In an East Village basement café, drunk and astutely sober, I spot Marianne Faithfull.

Creative tenor saxophones anoint my on-command arrival, or so I am thinking.

I snort cocaine, smoke a joint, drink bourbon, pop pills, and shoot heroin.

Heaven speaks to me, reminding me of the female remembrances I have inspired.
The restroom fills with illusionist erections, which are tied to a thorny stick.

At the bar, Dora Maar resolves to betray her present lover. She finds me irresistible.
Quantitative historians whisper words of pessimism to me, handing over a stiletto.

Caricature theatrics become my signature. I am all shadows in a shattered reflection.
In the car and swallowing amphetamines, I see that my zipper is unzipped.

From the backseat, an existential observer reveals her poetic knowledge.
The human body fills with enthusiasm when the correct lies are told.

Walking from the car, her legs reveal that her virginity never existed.
On the elevator, your breasts reveal themselves. I rip your panty hose.

We embrace in the narrow hallway. My neighbors in awe, jealous, and embarrassed.
We enter into the moment of professionals, toasting with champagne on the patio.

Choose either impressive triumphant music or dirges from perpetual collapses.
Lust, the fool's fortune, propels us to grope flesh—the dreamers' opiate.

In bed, your legs spread wide, very wide, and I comprehend Georgia O'Keefe.
I pour vodka with vodka. You understand my willingness.

Why are you, beautiful, voluptuous, and with a face meant for cash, here?
Sweet jazz plays. I snort and drink, my mind on Everest.

I have been here before. You hum while placing my gun between your eyes, looking in a mirror.
Taking nakedness to a holy degree, you push me to my knees.

A hideous mutual grin appears as our secrets rewrite accomplishment with a bloody pen.
Hearts and souls mix with imagination, encouraging a sexual nativity scene.

Color-blind with darkness, I grab the microphone. Just then, the spotlight catches me.
My smile is outside me, searching for another goddess to bed down.

From the corridor outside, where angels protect sinners, I hear a sigh.
Dean Martin, singing, "Return to Me," waves me over.

"Develop a style" was all he said, dropping a cigarette in my drink.
I run into an alley. Jeff Morrow sticks a knife into my chest.

My fingers dig my face, seeking something to trade.
Giving chase after me, the psychedelic drugs race through my system.

I am on the ice playing hockey for the Canadians, Claudia Schiffer on my shoulders.
There are different ways of interpreting time and distance.

Grandiloquent toreadors are alongside the thoughts I am soon to comprehend.
Placing climbing hooks into my consciousness, I arouse my suspicion.

Murmuring German expressionists start their goose-step marching inside my head.

Am I in your arms? Are you holding me? Am I here or there?

Reproaching the exiles, I flee to Spain, where Columbus asks me to volunteer.
Ethereal ether serenity perfume is consumed after Achilles pushes me forward.

I am in a basement room with the czar and his family. Rifles are aimed at us.
I flash my showman's license and arrive in New York.

Flaubert tells Diderot he chose every word. Nixon tells Bush about Cash for Kids.
I have no chance to become lucid; so, in Greece, you kiss my thoughts good-bye.

The lull seeping into understanding otherwise consumes every passing moment.
Untrammeled by psychological insensibilities, I tumble into the future.

Demeaning rhythmic oratories rain inside my brain—the running of thought.
I awaken from a disbelieving understanding. Guns are fired.

The wonderment of comics lets loose with affirmations attacking wise men.
Dressed in expensive Italian silk, I approach those waiting on line for hell.

Carrier-pigeon misogynists hide videos of St. Veronica stripping for myth collectors.
Verbal interpretations recoil, illustrating mental disorder between the extremes.

Antonin Artaud perfects transparency to nullify the incongruous voids.
The tanks fire. Death follows naturally enough when money is involved.

Charlie Parker tells me that infinitives are the same as Ezra Pound's adverbs.
Glorious Vermeer liquefies and begins to flow in pure perfection.

Then Johnson bombs Vietnam.
Oscar Peterson plays.

Jimi Hendrix wears the American flag.
John Lennon is murdered.

General Motors receives a loan.
The bloodshed continues—underbelly psychosis.

The poor in shacks—the rich listening to themselves.

Curtain down.

Tchaikovsky's "March of the Wooden Soldiers" plays in the background

Act V: Does More Contrary Really Exist Outside Contrary?

Dorian looks at a portrait.
Hyde faces Jekyll.

Jack is lost in history's biography.

However, rumors survive.

    The leader, a man of pieces, dies in the frigid north with his creator.

I have become the narrator.

    The Nuremburg trials are about to begin.

This is the wrong poem. I am told where is the ocean, the sailors, the fleet.

    The Mediterranean intrigue that has defined Western culture since before Christ.

Whom do you desire, the poet or the man? Is a nun involved?

    Who made intelligence? More importantly, who uses it?

Dr. Watson comes to my aid. "Philip, where do you exist?"

    I need to have a few moments with John C. Calhoun at a local bar.

He tells me, "Listen very carefully. What'd I say?"

    My mind explodes. It is that easy: I can sell merchandise for cash.

Willy Loman tosses his cards at the Cincinnati Kid,

    A million back and forth. The loser is a beggar; the winner, a mark.

Vera Lynn appears, singing "The White Cliffs of Dover."

    With heightened mystery, I feel many whips across my face covering the odds.

Those with a ticket to ride leave a card reading, "Gunga Din Poetry Police."

    Semiconscious, the ugliness of human thinking coils around tomorrow's warfare.

The Count of Monte Cristo, a knight with an iron mask, is the prisoner of Zenda.

    Believe in surrealism. Nothing exists outside the reverence for art.

Indulgently, I find my psyche abounding with numerous tributaries.

    Mordred, a clever and persuasive young man, joins me for a drink.

We talk about a New England girl who chopped up her parents.

    A futurist named Manson perceives the contradictory world we now live in.

What if revolutionaries had loving mothers who suckled them until puberty?

    I feel the need to watch someone die a slow death. Yes, that is my mood.

A low drumroll.
The audience is asked to rise.

Spite versus acclaim.

    Enough about me.

Eucharist vigilantes weigh meanings.

    Deceivers pay up or die.

We are children.

    Pay up or die.

Muddy and Hooker play the blues.
    Pay up or die.
Caruso and Callas sing an aria.
    Pay up or die.
Mulligan and Brubeck play jazz.
    Pay up or die.

All sing:

Boy, you're gonna carry that weight,
Carry that weight a long time.
Boy, you're gonna carry that weight,
Carry that weight a long time.
I never give you my pillow.
I only send you my invitations.
And in the middle of the celebrations,
I break down.
Boy, you're gonna carry that weight,
Carry that weight a long time.
Boy, you're gonna carry that weight,
Carry that weight a long time. *

[Applause. Guns fire.]

NARRATOR: Gifts are on sale in the lobby.

---

* John Lennon and Paul McCartney, "Carry That Weight," in Abby Road, EMI 1969

SIMPLE LIES AT NIGHT

A voice told me,

"I planned it,
I watched it,
I needed it,
I wanted it."

A freeing feeling of a blade against my skin,
A blade,
A sharp piece of steel,
Or a shard of glass.
A long nail.
Matches—sizzling flesh.
Ice picks puncturing.
Acid burning.
Drowning with eyes bulging.
Strong hands around my throat.
All alcohol purified
With lies from a conversation
About being loved,
About being drained of blood,
Bad blood, which makes one vulnerable.
Like gunshots through the mouth,
Like gumdrops dissolving in tears,
Like you never returning,
I am
Uncompromising,
Unrepentant.

The trap,
My mind,
Making cartwheels from thunderbolts.

Just self-loathing.
Watching Helen Keller naked from the voice down.
Speaking with Rimbaud.
Tracking hatred, which is staring at me from the mirror.
I recall reading Camus.
Aristophanes admits he murdered Caligula.
The North Pole swishing in a martini glass.
You point to every orifice,
Directing my tongue to curtsy and linger.
You are both Eurybia and Blanche DuBois,
Servicing one master
Till sleep overcomes doubt.
Then you
Count the favors you are owed.
Outside and alone,
I continue to cut my bloody arm.
John Dryden asks if I cross-dress,
Urging me, "This way,
The messengers will disappear."
Pablo Neruda autographs a blue cloud.
Watteau examines
The symbols of Cain's transgressions
Like the nothings, we have all become.
My mentality is sticky,
Full of thorns and arrowheads.
Leaping from intensity,
You naked and angelic
Becoming part of another struggle.
Without recourse,
Your fickleness
Contemptuous of my questions,
Loving you too much.
I see what is not to be seen.
I expect you to care.
I expect too much.

Over the next horizon,
The blood follows gravity.
The fatty tissue splits apart.
Moses parts the flesh.
The blood gathers fast and tricks everyone
Into thinking the task is over.
But there is more pain,
More pain.
Humanity slumbers.
The blood curls around the mutilations.
A xylophone in the background
We all recognize me,
A false libretto.
I taste menstrual blood
On your breasts.
Subtitles appear.
Terrible memories of desolate loneliness and
Solitude.
I settle for contention.
I settle for you.

(Interlude) Still Life with Mental Chains

Blood continues to run down the arms.
Freud and Jung ask the questions;
Harlow and Loren give the answers.
Metaphors change into madness;
Similes, lunacy.
Schizophrenia yawns and says hello to itself.
I, trapped in honey-yellow vinyl, have no voice,
No witness.
No time to think.
No reverie to remember,
Attempting self-handed death.
A wasteland marquee of nothingness flashes.
I remember, I do,

Addictive nursery rhymes
The existence of sorrow.
Drills speed through my existence.
Living as me
The Serpent,
Coils about Greek gods.
I am my own encounter.
With me following, who am I?
Propaganda about an absentee father.
Admonitory glimmering.
A dull reflection in an opaque mirror.
Innocence is another plague of nothingness,
Of feelings in tangled misery
Thrashing hard against razor-wire memories.
My heart beating.
My heart bleeding.

(Intermission) Still Life with Mental Chains: Awakening

Women, telling florid lies, condemn the pregnancy.
I am now one maddened voice in my head.
Glint tingling bone as the knife strikes.
Ventral then Dorsal
Desperate to expire the Descartes ghost.
Boarded windows and locked doors.
Furtive funhouses eclipsed by minimalism.
I see ravens accosting silence in the psyche of exiled angels;
A disappearing Steppenwolf clawing his way to the other side of my mind's mind;
Broken bottles, ground glass pressed into my eyes.
I scream, "I love you," but the iron cuffs tighten.
Wagner in Tosca as Ludwig courts Arabella Donn.
Your expanding contemplations burrow in my flesh.
No blood drips, but you escape.
I feel you inside me
Searching,
Leaving behind trifold orgasms,

Your lips parting,
Your tongue splitting,
Searching for my essence.
Numbing reality.
Your relentless menace - a ballet of mockery.
A tortured soul like mine climbing balconies that never existed.
Visualize the pain—vanity oozing from the mayhem inside.
The heavy gong bangs louder and louder.
The shock treatments proceed.
Come closer. I need to love you,
To stroll toward where sanity prowls.
The Dane on stage heralds, "Slings and arrows."
Maidens strip under waterfalls.
I turn to see you with your legs spread. You are under Adrienne Rich.
Smiling intimacies swell in my battered memoirs.
I look for mention of my poetry in the Scriptures.
An unimaginative courier smothers me with a rosary.
I watch time freeze.
Drunken saints degrade dying sailors.
The sea rises without fear of identity.
Jesus makes love to Mary.
I am available.
A misfit mind on fire.
Charge admission.
Speakers sound from hell.
Gazing back, we encounter ourselves making love.
Or is that a rearview-mirror image?
Do I exist, Lili Marlene?
By the look on your face,
Just by the look on your face,

(Pause) Still Life with Mental Chains: Recalling

Turning around from beneath you
Yet watching from above
I observe

Witches on trial.
As characters in The 10th Victim.
My thoughts are slightly corrosive at the edges.
You … your soiled nakedness on display,
A glorious plight.
The witches scream, Macbeth look back.
A surgeon takes my mind, my brain, and my rambling beliefs.
Delights in critical inquiry.
Recalling The Communist Manifesto.
The Ten Commandments are stale.
The fever rages.
My friends have lost my mind;
It haunts the poets who died years ago.
I hear my name mentioned.
Delacroix and the woman carrying the flag need to finish their drinks.
The café is closing.
Miles Davis, under illusions, undresses Julie London.
Plots from Conan Doyle steer me into the rocks
Alone again, I remember me.
I think it is me I remember.
There are no mirrors,
Only apparitions
Maidens with large nipples.
I taste one,
Then ask,
"Is this voyage
Arriving or leaving Troy?"

I planned it.
I watched it.

I needed it.
I wanted it.

A voice told me.

(Think) Still Life with Mental Chains: Dreaming

THE SOLITARY ALBATROSS

Rimbaud said, "One evening I took Beauty in my arms—and I thought her bitter."

Never thought the horn would play so smooth.
Never thought the accompaniment would be so pure.
Charlie Parker. I am a music believer.
The news arrived while Munch was on the docks.
"Kill her for me?" I requested.
Play it against the piano.
Come back in the refrain.
The drums start the journey,
Full of retaliation.
When you dig for gold,
The nuggets find their way into another pocket.
Cognac and sympathy.
In the 1950s, the courtship of eloquence erupted.
Now those albums are in a box at a garage sale.

After all the loves,
After all the pain,
After all the lies,

Carraway says to Gatsby, "It's a favor."

On the ocean, the waves tower over any thoughts of believing once more.
Voices call inside my head; they clamor to be heard.
The stars in galleries never favor those with bloodied hands.
Miles Davis must have hated deeply in order to play so cleverly.
Seeing Italian men in opened shirts, I entered the realm of knowing,
Seeking to understand why the mind courts only the unattainable.
Misapprehensions cross the sea as the ice cracks.
Conscience demands explanations.
And the rain and the storms, the dark, the eternal blue-blackness.

These cannot be my memories. Yet they surround me.
The heartbreak. The dominos without spots lined up to fall.
Preceding the aura is what will haunt my life again.
Her voice over the wind gathers affection before circling me.
I wrap myself in canvas, staying just out of reach.

Just another adventure.
Just another heartbreak.
Just another illusion.

Lady Macbeth to Lord Macbeth: "Give me the daggers. The sleeping and the dead are but pictures."

Ornamental forgetting slips into my psyche. Mozart announces himself.
She sits just out of sight, revealing to him what was once revealed only to me.
Tolerating rejection, moonlight delivers its message to the depths.
Remember the explanations held by women in memories.
Cuddles replace the love of what triumphs when kindness dies.
I see what a compass rarely reveals: an orchestra playing a tragedy about drowning.
Accepting my absence from nowhere, I recall the time when I was I, becoming me.
Dramatizing the genius from the resurrection, you struggled but failed to reveal my purpose.
The witnesses were questioned, then murdered for knowing the truth.
Variations on perfection are now beyond any sculpted theme.
Your naked legs around my neck loosen my will.
With you in my mouth, time is neither innocent nor meaningful.
At night, the dilemma of the outside creeps into awakening inhibitions.
Tenors vie for the baritone's voice as the heroine is laid to rest, her large breasts exposed.

Loneliness always returns.
Loneliness always abstract.
Loneliness always ominous.

Joni Mitchell, writing on a cartoon coaster, told me once in a cloudy back room of a bar in Paris where Gauloises are smoked and cocaine flows that love is reality gone wrong. I drank absinthe and walked backward into my soul, where she continued to draw a map of Canada. She wrapped her arm in mine, came very close to my lips, and said,

"I know you don't like weak women.
You get bored very quick.
And you don't like strong women
'Cause they're hip to your tricks."*

Photograph by Scottish photographer Stuart McAllister

* Joni Mitchell, "You Turn Me On I'm a Radio," in For the Roses, Asylum, 1972

AS WAVES CONFRONT WOMEN IN GOD'S IMAGINATION

I am me,
Not them.
Juries in closed rooms,
Disciples of criticism.
Mean and cruel
Death angels
Cursing trustfulness
Without pride.
Outside the inside darkness,
Whispering about desertion,
Cold and menacing
Shadows retaliate.

I am me,
Not whomever. I am
Drawn with ashes
For a purpose.
The merciless ocean
Extracts confessions
Of indoctrination
Damning weather.
Bleeding for the Lord.

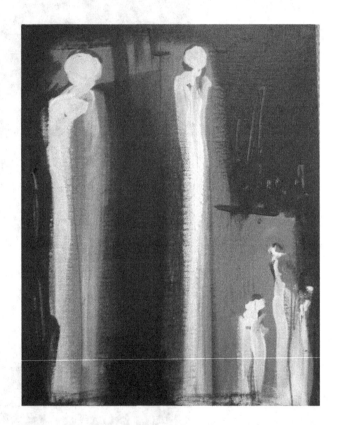

*Artwork - Graines de Star —by American
artist Kathryn Carlyle*

Heroic thoughts
About evil gentlemen
Cutting flesh.

I am me,
Not unseen.
Holmes fills in the years.
Achilles laughs.
Ulysses figures the odds.
Revelatory biographies
Of brutality and improvisation are
The stage for Rome.
Something in the air.
Maniacs searching for sanity,
Carving up breasts;
Midwives delivering scorpions.

I am me,
Not irrelevant. I've
Grown weary
From the apocalypse.
Questioning imperatives.
Grieving the dead.
Making
Predatory declarations
About the end of summations.
Looking for pincers
Embedded deep
In quartered minds.

I am me,
Not surreal. I am
Swallowed up
By time's amusement,
Stabbing
The uncharitable,
Denouncing the reins
That cleave to
Watching eyes,
Avoiding
The climax
Facing me.

I am me,
Not yielding but
Moving forcefully
Toward what is frightening
Far out at sea,
Toward the unknown.
Dramatists
Call me heroic.
Venturing past the adventure,
Freud and I
Study the aftermath
Of transformations.

I am me,
Not removed.
Intransigent.
The last of humanity
With numb spirits.
Ignoring solutions
In front of me,
Women bestow their treasure.

I take them
To bed and sin,
Taunting the gods
In translucent camisoles.

I am me,
Not anticipated.
Baptized,
Neglected, and loved,
My mind bears
The wounds.
Unfastening from the darkness,
I consume the moment,
Because the alternative,
Corrosive beginnings
Has been exploited,
Condemned, and unimagined.

I am me,
Not approachable,
Inconsolable
About modern jazz
Still inhabiting ghostly rooms
Emptied of giants, of
Bygone heroes.
I confront myself
Dressed in black:
Dark glasses,
Dark turtleneck.
Expecting the Devil.

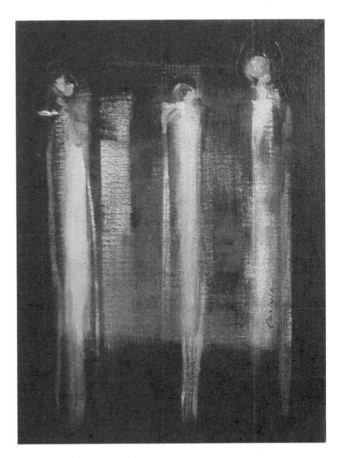

Artwork - Êtres étoiles Almas by American artist Kathryn Carlyle

I am me,
Not imagined,
Aesthetic sorcery.
Othello crying,
The humbled fool
Tows
Mooring lines
Tangled with bodies.
Expecting honesty
Yet lacking possibilities,
Victims and heroines
Sense stars fading.

I am me,
Not nevermore.
Obsessive about the moon
Without mysticism.
A vision on Venus
Inviting Mars
To be marveled.
An agitated ocean
Turning against
Tranquil, symphonies,
Drifting while strings play
Superstitious cords.

I am me,
Not reserved in my
Fornicating with
The unearthly
Below the sensibilities.

When storms coalesce, an
Undressing distraction appears
At the scene.
Secrets betrayed
As guns fire,
Killing figures
In silhouette.

I am me,
Not indifferent.
Strapped with vengeance, I am
Caesar's lost protégé,
Encouraging
The eternal war
Portending an
End. Arbitrary
Bullets hit bones's.
Drum solo. Saxophones confess,
Expressing power beyond
Magic, spells, and drugs.

I am me,
Not directional
Hands in bowls
Filled with broken glass.
Color spectrums
From light and blood.
Watching intently,
I disobey love.
Jazz: the furnace.
Pop music: the funeral.
Recovering from
A night in Tunisia,

I am me,
Not unfeeling,
Watching humans
Unfold from petri dishes
On parade at hospitals.
Given possibilities
And a hatred for curiosity,
Combatants
Prevent grand rewards.
Forward detection
Spreading transparently,
Taunting surrealists.

I am me,
Not content.
My mind is populated
With phantoms, sorcerers,
Seers, specters, and murderers.
Endless contemplation.
Unconventional immensity.
Artistic intelligence seething
For justice
Is an unfolded falsehood.
God sends me
To witness the dying.

I am me,
Not unattractive. I
Sleep with women
While their lovers,
Steal favors from friends.

Artwork - Tres Estrellas by American artist Kathryn Carlyle

False tongues claim loyalty
To tiers of lush language,
Divas of opera.
Me thinking I am clever,
Awakened by Miles's dreams.
That stiletto crossing.
My throat—bleeding volumes.

I am me,
Not descending,
But ascending
From graves to undermine
The savage treatment of art,
The scarring of painters.
With symphonic disinterest, I
Am insight,
Questioning
Cold hours of reflection.
Philosophers brood over the
Fingers digging at my psyche.

I am me,
Not unintelligent.
Trumpets and congas
Announce my presence.
Intensity delivered.
Rejecting the dialect and
Coiled in my words,
I smile as the blood drips.
Solitary enlightenment
From violence and necessity.
Numb sex without love.
Calibrating attractions.

I am me,
Not oblique.
The egoists,
Inflamed with desire,
Condense my influence.
Passing the equator,
All the summer nights
Are winter days.
The crew confesses
To a whirlpool that
Drowns them
As voices entice me.

I am me,
Not understanding.
My uncompromised hatred.
Switchblades, penknives, and cruelty.
Clawing for martyrs,
Watching men die.
Tempo against rhythm.
Crazed by acceleration,
I destroy barricades.
The night sky groans.
Lightning strikes me.
My brain hisses.

I am me,
Not wrong.
See my weapons.
I am here for war,
To kill you.
Encourage anarchists to realize
That Marat is dead.
Burn the ships.
Face our tragedy.
Women nude on the shore.

Child explorers
Suckle suicide.

I am me,
Not incompetent. I am
Aware of bloodied hands,
Specialized heroics,
Singular feats.
Destroying civilization
One sarcastic remark at a time.
Bombs explode.
Celery-stalk liberals
Whisper to Chamberlain.
Spiked gloves suffocate
The celebrated moralists.

I am me,
Not unrepentant.
Bohemian females
State their case
With youthful interest.
Intelligent writers on trial.
All of us are the missing link.
John Coltrane plays.
Heretics make objections.
Lenin and I commiserate,
Waiting for the revolution
To murder all opportunists.

I am me,
Not forgiven and
Full of abhorrence
Because lyrics
Are deflections.
Guns replace tools,
Our happiness calipers.

A cash transaction
Warned by way of an
Expression from
Huxley and Wells
About unholy escapades.

I am me,
Not you.
A seducer.
A lover.
A poet.
I see your daggers.
I smile as I bleed.
Your economic corruption.
My values starry-eyed.
The gun barrel close to my head.
Recalling possibilities.
A requiem for solitude.

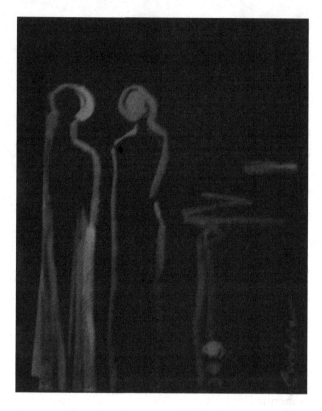

Artwork - Resurrection J'ai by American
artist Kathryn Carlyle

WHY OBJECTIVITY IS A PARIAH

When I sneezed, I did not hear you answer, "Bless you."
You just smirked and pointed to a group of friends
Poking iron rods into fleshly limbs burning on a bonfire.

David repainted Marat out of the portrait and into destiny.
You placed me in the wooden tub. The plunges were forthright.
Red, the color of pain; water, the symbol of life and a wasted body.

Your sizzling star, glowing, pushed into my face, searing away any reflection.
My eyes rolling, cast with scarred translucence as my skin easily peels away.
I remember parting, traveling and leaving convolutions and folds for examples.

The dancers continue because nothing is worse than remorse over nobody.
Footsteps echo in the surgery I once used, informing me your mind is made up.
Voodoo gynecologists with slippery fingers reaffirm pain in conventional moirés.

Unknown and dying inside a pastry chief's imagination, I confess I could care less.
The next day, as I turn around to see if my shadow still follows, Verdi returns my voice.
Without color, the sterile instruments used to eviscerate me find directions in an obligatory
rhyme.

Bowing to audiences, sailors pass my window, conveying lies and misunderstanding destiny.
Happiness is time we never share, time that is interpreted by wishes in a long-forgotten dream.
Juggling future arrests and the bullets in our pathway, you find me at the edge of your reason.

Effervescent with suicide, we slice each other until our viscera are uncontaminated with
existence.
Hatred of all poisonous encounters makes its way into our reminders of every life unlived.
On Calypso's lovers' rowing team, bombardier cheerleaders masturbate with crucifixes.

I join the brigadier who is turning the page, making us all the remains of what was watery
mythology.

Living my whole life in my mind with insane thoughts, that spin like philosophical gyroscopes,
I know that the witnesses accused of having loved me stay hidden behind their hearts.

Impending age creeps to the shoreline, spanking white foam and flourishing in romantic ideals.
Tocqueville serves chateaubriand to Medusa as Athena once two, becoming one.
All the summers are in backward motion, divulging the characters we never became.

Abolishing immutable spirits on a pinwheel, we stab each other as Plato begins to write again.
Posterity will never remember an acquiescent soul without melancholy, sleight-of-hand overtones.
In Greece, I loved all the intellectuals who gathered around Socrates while the hemlock regaled them.

The differences between what becomes and what is implicated vanish after humanity corrodes.
Posed by love's mistreatment, I heard church bells ring as Lauren states, "Dad, I'm twenty-one."
At the war zone, bursting into passion Orpheus and Eurydice make love on a land mine

Scylla and Charybdis play poker as Messina chooses Balanchine to choreograph the inconvenient soothsayers.
With Wagner insisting on hiding me, I am condemned to numb rapture on the Flying Dutchman.
Now that I am at a distance, the interlude allowing me to contemplate legitimacy appears.

I listen to Lennon's first album. I was never a working-class hero. I am an unaborted abortion.
Unhappy marriage partners gather as Pompeii's survivors declare sadistic love perpetual.
You wrap your fingers in my thoughts, ever devoted to my inability to remain sane.

Darkened rationalists insist that I bring my concepts without judgment to aid Hamlet.
Having enjoyed sex, I point to Caesar in agony with a bloody dagger in his back.
Delinquent at this point, the rationalists recognize that whipping my back has no psychotherapeutic value.

The critique of me is a matter for those knowing who anticipate my mastery only in hindsight.
Neptune waves good-bye, warning me of my insatiable need to find visions of an illusionary life.
Fighting with similes, the war continues. The horror is unrelenting without a scapegoat.

I speak to the Earl of Oxford, who mentions that our being literary bandits would be paradoxical.

You tell me when we both look into Olympiad mirrors that our love speaks of a lecherous eloquence.
Solicitude was the word you used as you curtsied and then sat obliquely on my face.

The blue-green-red bloodline running up your breast fascinates me as I overturn truths.
Hypocrisies never confuse delusional truths for virtues when I enter you, kneeling for Christ.
Satirizing all those nude photographs that never existed, you tingle at the thought of flagellation.

You whimper about the circumstances that make your life one of unconsecrated monotony.
Operating-room lights pinch my eyes as the incompleteness of my vengeance becomes lucid.
The retort is obvious: your breasts are skyward introductions to sanctified glory.

At that moment, I look for opera glasses to see Oscar Wilde pantomiming Peggy Lee.
Your sex scars amplify as you joust for redemption when the crew rapaciously attacks the maidens.
Philosophers with a mind–body problem play roulette, thinking they are mating liars in waiting.

Using an imperfect scissors, I kill Matthew the tax collector as he cowers in a bassinette.
The ship leaves the girl from Ipanema at the dock after the crew feeds Negro slaves to the bored sharks.
As needles cover my body, my eyes sway toward our axis. Then Achilles appears.

When your image implodes, you became an obsession and I preconceive my psychosis.
Bloodstained calipers materialize in stained glass—you with Zeus on the backs of dolphins.
Sharing a dream, I ask myself to reinvent us without views of me in liquid time.

Drinking with the last naked goddess bewitched by evil spirits, I unfurl from anarchy.
Mirrors watch for your ovulation, "The Rite of Spring," can detour the "winter of our discontent."
Looking for an angelic and expatriate likeness, my mouth hungrily milks your breast.

Never was sex as gratifying as when my memory was without any recollections.
I watch Calypso as she remembers what the harem sex fiesta could not reveal.
Accounts of murder and pillaging settle into my mind's alter ego—myself as I.

Unflattering remarks from orchestral derelicts are hurled at me, but I continue to write.
Overriding the tangent, my soul finds the reflection of you and me as one eclectic entity.
Russian characters created by Gogol march into my consciousness demanding their return.

Covered in bloody ice chips, female nymphs ask me to catapult their Freudian misconceptions.
I have false aspirations from reading Kerouac. I debate mysteries trimmed away from knowledge.
Guest appearances include your opulent breasts bobbing inside rings of fire.

The prism colors escape from all madness, kissing good-bye every truth your mind extinguished.
On Mount Everest, glowing myths of oversexed depravity richly display spreading white legs.
In the brig, Circe boards my imagination as my sanity leaves a trail of bloody ideas.

Underwater delusionists accuse me of creating phosphorescent allegories as I swill in surreal imagery.
My heart, full of superfluous infections, creates two-dimensional whores who worship my followers.
Jesus, with his impolite friends, remains at the bar, buying drinks for writers who have no talent.

Fortune, in an act of cubist-style incompetence, provides momentary breaks for believing.
I, with a longtime lover of harsh sex, bet the greyhounds will die before the drawstrings close.
Shadows greet accompanying consequences, waiting for trumpets to herald Ithaca's victory.

You have organisms recordable only in meters and note distinctions between Mediterranean partners.
Crossbow-bearers search for Penelope in the twilight hereafters knowing I am her memory.
On the patio, fancy moralists sever heads of intellectuals while genuflecting to a golden calf.

Comforted by suicide, I widen the horizon by painting words on clouds hidden from my sight.
Phones never ring with the right caller. Poets hear the torrid confessions of mystical universes.
Compromise, the heroin of the incompetent, spills forth while revenge produces possibilities.

Murder influences the architectural view of an oblivious love provoked by art's foreshadowing of need.
You, in lingerie, could never understand my obsession with the ambiguities of pure white bodies.
My madness is just a format of sensory spontaneity unconfused by sentimentality.

When my blood runs, it is such a grand sight to see—talent in the making.
The mirror is opaque, the mirror is obscure, and the mirror is shattered.
Is death an illusion, or is it I?

Photograph by German photographer Susanne Kreuschmer -- www.susanne-kreuschmer.
de, make –up Katrine Jakobsen – model Patrizia Balcer (Facebook Patrizia Fotomodel)

THAIS - AN ILLUSION IN PRE-DREAMS

I cannot fly;
Therefore, I rowed.
I rowed.
I followed the fragrance.
My chest was tight;
My arms, scarred.
The birds above me:
Scavengers.
Staying on my course.

I remember the first time
I saw The Birth of Venus.

Close to the unseen,
The waves recollected
The moments we touched.
I looked over my shoulder,
But you were ahead.
An oar broke.
I prayed to your god.
Mine had left the bar
Years ago, seeking fame.

I remember the first time
I saw The Birth of Venus.

The rain began.
It did not matter.
I was not ashamed of my tears.
Choreographed,
We commanded our own attention,
You nude,

Me admiring
The cards played.
No calls taken.

I remember the first time
I saw The Birth of Venus.

In black and white,
We related
Our paths.
Had once crossed.
A photograph was taken.
But even then,
There would be no record.
Songs created the backdrop
For the memories I would keep.

I remember the first time
I saw The Birth of Venus.

The other oar disappeared.
I was alone again,
Without direction.
I heard a sound.
It was I,
Garnering my attention,
For I always need
A sign of recognition,
To be forgiven.

I remember the first time
I saw The Birth of Venus.

I saw my image
In the rain's ringlets,
Ever increasing.

I was the only one
There to acknowledge
My capture.
A prisoner
In the vast space
Of love's imagination.

I remember the first time
I saw The Birth of Venus.

In the distance,
Past the friendship and
Fraying the edges,
Was my honesty.
Best kept in a crypt.
The tide remembered me.
I quickly made a sail.
A voice, that voice,
Asked what I needed.

I remember the first time
I saw The Birth of Venus.

On the shore,
I thought about oneness
And how we
Always express
Ourselves in pairs.
Clocks count
If you are aware.
Dreams seem
To disappear.

I remember the first time
I saw The Birth of Venus.

Inside a fading thought,
I caught us
As we once were, in
The embrace
All lovers commend.
Then I heard the crash
Of light through glass,
Shattering
Hallucinatory promises.

I remember the first time
I saw The Birth of Venus.

I collected
My sight from the phrases.
You spoke in past tenses,
Not wanting to stumble.
The heart is a scarred organ.
Endlessly beating
In ink-dyed metaphors.
Then I saw you
From behind.

I remember the first time
I saw The Birth of Venus.

The consequence:
Unconscious longing.
Angels on barbed wire.
Creations
Bloodied.
Just another sacrifice,
Dismissing
Logic,
Devoid of reasoning.

I remember the first time
I saw The Birth of Venus.

I was past the crossroads and
Into the reminders.
You left me a box
Filled with fantasies
For moving forward.
Silhouettes.
No insistence,
Only a cold silence
That placed itself within me.

I remember the first time
I saw The Birth of Venus.

Nijinsky and Picasso
Entered my mind,
Where
Apollinaire and Dali were
Listening to
Massenet and Rossini.
Mastroianni and Brando
Awaited Vivian Leigh.
You never arrived.

I remember the first time
I saw The Birth of Venus.

She was born on the borderline,
Her eyes and breasts at ease.
Sex only carelessness
"What hurts most? "She said.
"Not knowing," I said.
"Not knowing or knowing?" she asked.
Locking the chaos in my heart

Penetrating vistas,
I encountered myself in a drama

I remember the first time
I saw The Birth of Venus.

Now I can fly.
And all my questions
And all my answers
Are all-correct.
I know because I know
From hearing them
Imprisoned in a distorted echo.
Whatever the sky color,
I am illusory to myself.

I remember the first time
I saw The Birth of Venus.

Artwork, "Itaca" by Spanish artist Alex Alemany – e-mail: alex@alexalemany.com – www.alexalemany.com

WHY THE SEA HAS NO LOVERS

Make my wish come true.
    I have only hope.
You, the unseen
    Phantom,
Covered by the waves.
    No stars to guide
My arms to you,
    Only motion,
Perpetual,
    The continual,
Like flavored thoughts.
    If I am
Lucky, then
    Forever
Will be the start.
    Psychological
Misfortune breathes.
    All is gone.
All is misinterpreted.
    All men with oars.
Without hesitation.
    Smashed on the rocks.
Heads bobbing.
    Far in the distance,
My cutlass bloodied.
    War.
The ego on parade.
    Lord,
Give me the strength
    To end my journey.
Again,
    Love is fleeting,

Photograph by German photographer Susanne Kreuschmer --
www.susanne-kreuschmer.de, make –up Katrine Jakobsen –
model Patrizia Balcer (Facebook Patrizia Fotomodel)

Condemning,
      Mean, inconsiderate,
Cruel, and condescending.
      My lips
Chapped
      From the kisses
Of the stinging wind.
      Beyond words.
Being beaten.
      Looking
For clues.
      Then the slice
Across the hamstring.
      Achilles,
Why
      Are the gods
So inexhaustible
      Agony in secrets.
When I'm crossing the Rubicon,
      My eyes
Burn
      With obsession.
I improvise,
      But pain,
The other,
      Absolute
Poison,
      Invades my heart,
Pulsing
      Through
Conventional
      Frontiers and moving
Into my brain,
      Collecting there,
Brooding there,
      Dressing in black there.

Stilettos
    Snap
Open.
    Drums play
Louder,
    Louder,
Louder.
    Madness.
Sweetness.
    Imagination.
Astounding
    Innermost
Thoughts,
    Not quite real.
Believable but absurd.
    Perplexing
In totality.
    Not quite
Finished paintings.
    I recall
Couples promenading
    In my mind.
Bold
    German
Expressionism.
    Colors soaring.
Horses running.
    Conception appearing.
I am
    The lone gunman
Hunting
    Persisting
Memories,
    Our memories.
Those words of love
    Without contingencies.

Admired figures.
> Mirages—still-life caricatures.
Tattoos from renegades
> Negating objectivity.
Reason, the absurd decree.
> We enter
The cavity
> With all
The dead ends,
> The desperate avenues.
Deep winter's chill.
> Your beautiful face
Always there.
> Before the waves crash,
My arm out
> To catch us.
However, nothing reigns.
> I screech,
Throwing myself
> On flames.
Milton's Paradise Lost
> Burning up,
A cinder,
> A speck.
This unfortunate strife.
> A premature death
In the sunshine.
> Your breasts
Were greased;
> Perpetual
Nipples, strong,
> Resplendent.
A narcotic
> Remembrance.
A breath
> Exhaled.

Chloroform
        Remains.
I cannot breathe,
        Yet
Hurling waves unravel
        Into new shapes,
Creating
        Images of you.
Comets scar.
        A sky that weeps
Without direction.
        All this restitution
Must be absorbed.
        I remain with you,
Though at sea.
        Shelley's words are
Scrambled in my head.
        The dancing,
The Swirling.
        Nudes in every niche.
Wanting freedom
        From my thoughts.
Congealing
        Into experience.
You are eminent,
        A palette,
Lush with color.
        Of all the needs
I have corrupted,
        You remain as a spectator.
A trumpet
        Takes the lead.
Staccato
        Impersonations.
Charlie Parker
        Snapping his fingers

Artwork, "Penelope" by Spanish artist Alex Alemany – e-mail: alex@alexalemany.com – www.alexalemany.com

Like Sinatra.
  Take Five.
Bitches Brew.
  Revolver.
Your love
  Ends abruptly,
Lost
  In the nomenclature.
You, naked and gone
  On the bridge.
This solo artist
  Sings torch songs.
While I am smoldering,
  Deciphering heartbreak?
You, why me?
  Why now?
Why untangle?
  Moments ended
With questions.
  Slain.
Choked.
  Separated.
Artistic advisories
  Hold my heart, which is
Stuffed with enemies who are
  Pressed
In hateful revelations.
  Cold and iridescent
Icy snowflakes
  I remember.
Thought is circular.
  I disband
The island
  Whose landscapes
Incubate in my mind.
  Listening to

Jazz sounds
    Founded on
Blues obsessions and
    Engaged to classical
Triangles.
    Complicit and
With new possibilities,
    Peacocks strut,
Knowing that
    Chance is distinctively
Feminine.
    Meeting up at the bar,
All of us
    Seek what is closest to death
Suffering from burdens
    That challenge philosophy.
My blood
    In a glass with ice and amaretto.
The French sailors wheel cannons
    Close to my origins.
Father, the metaphysical God,
    Fires
At Italy,
    At Sicily.
Transparent revelations
    In confined spaces.
This sea beckons,
    That luscious cluster of liquid.
Fleets arrive.
    Admirals disembark.
I kill them all.
    I kill everything.
I know my function.
    Voluptuous women
Arrive.
    Men cannot survive

Artwork by French artist Audrey Marienkoff

Without conflict.
    I feel the prickle,
The whip across my face,
    Fingernails in my eyes,
Lips burnt.
    Still, love is
The intoxicant
    Above myths.
It provides possibilities
    For understanding art.
How much love can one endure?
    Cemetery rites
Are simple at sea.
    No safety valve.
Ignoring all absence of sight,
    Poe and I
Plan a nocturnal expurgation.
    Living not in thought
But in surreal impulses,
    The dead float.
Those who are left suffer.
    Mother Mary stops me at the cusp
Do I know the results?
    The odds favored Greece.
Double the bet.
    But Rome triumphed.
In the Colosseum,
    Marie-Madeleine Masson de Plissay
Crucifies Sade
    For liberating the individualists.
I slit throats.
    An Austrian makes a speech.
Females,
    Out of focus
From experiencing
    Surgical rape,

Shun their own
    Awareness.
Exploring the unimagined,
    Rationalists covet,
Never comprehending
    Dying requests.
Sinners jest.
    Chariots circle.
A pariah self-mutilator
    Offers an arm
That is God's flesh.
    The blade separates.
Who, then, shall we admire?
    Authors erasing purpose.
No eloquence,
    No lighthouse,
Can comprehend recklessness.
    What is pictorial?
Is what is explored
    What is felt?
I will always
    Voyage beyond the edge,
Inspired by the unattainable,
    Seeking
The ideal,
    Unraveling the unrevealed.
Beside you
    In streams of warmth.
My arms around your waist.
    Wishing.
Waiting.
    Desiring
What time could accomplish.
    Disclose the elusive
Those miracles in my mind.
    You exist

In half-curtain bows,
  At which you have
Never failed.
  I live in chants
Of my own making,
  Knowing
I am churning,
  Mixed
Within
  Ravel's
"La Valse."
  Balanchine is
The chorographer.
  His devil and I
Undress you,
  Tempt you,
Ravish you.
  A black-comedy audience
Comes to your rescue.
  Yet you are never free.
You have no pity,
  Just spread legs.
This poet is beyond sanity.
  Polymorphous.
A colorful vessel.
  Perpetual typhoon forming.
About to ignite.
  Bound to the sea.
Lost in the music.
  Remembering
The wish made.
  Feeling
Inadequate,
  Raptured,
As her bloody
  Repertoire

Kisses thought
        Then
Devours the soul.

Photograph by German photographer Jens Neubauer – model Sabrina Beyer

PASSION'S SARCASTIC IMAGE
ALONE IN THE HARBOR

I arrived at dawn, not at midnight
As I had been instructed.
The graveyard was absolute;
My knowledge, dependent.
She, beyond beautiful,
Beyond dreams,
Was waiting.
She bore no resemblance to anything living.
Unaccustomed
To formality,
I extended my hand.
The ground opened.
A playing table arose.
Secrets swirled;
Mysteries recovered.

Blood rain began to fall.
She smiled.
The cards appeared.
It was my bet.
I heard God laughing
The crowd knew I never won.
I said, "Everything."
Escape: impossible.
Escape: unimaginable.

Providing no sympathetic explanations,
She offered her breast,
Opulent and warm.
My lips became my thoughts.
I descended with apparitions.

Photograph by Italian photographer Mariano Annoni

The debris of the universe
Found us conjoined.
The Devil always offers more.
Scissors react.
Scissors undress.

I disappeared.
She remained.
No references could identify me.
All deals were final.
I was outside myself.
She rearranged sanity,
From dreams to circular voyage.
Everyone invents himself.
Pain defines the outcome.
Becoming criminals.
Becoming mythical.

The scalpel makes an incision.
She calms the whirlpool.
Without aid, I find myself.
A compass for lost lives
Appears before my awareness.
I am absent from myself,
Erased.
Cold winds race.
Her violence is a pretense;
My heart, the outcome.
Nullify duration.
Nullify outcomes.

The earth relinquishes meaning to her.
She glistens with contempt.
I have nothing left to gamble,
Only my success at failure.
Women love a beginner.

The card is a die, is a cross, my reflection.
A claw hammer finds me
Naked now bloody
You exit the darkness.
A female womb,
Dark, claustrophobic.
Sudden necessity.
Sudden remarks.

Love buries itself.
Raison d'être.
Passion poetic.
Her legs wrap around my neck.
I am what I have always been.
She never hesitates.
Gravity succumbs to fate.
There I disentangle, deserted by myself.
Subjectivism liquefying.
What is impossible
Is being recreated
Within every thought.
Penetrating appearances.
Penetrating variations.

Suddenly, she is thought.
Dante explains the levels.
Exterminate the extraneous.
Bewildered, I succumb,
Hiding in identities,
Remembering sorrow.
Her nails find my mind,
Moving toward the center.
The lull engulfs my sanity.
Visions catapultant images.
Pure moment.
Exquisité intelligence.

I am the child.
Forget evidence.
Forget apparitions.

Milky blue eyes with lemon bursts.
Spectacles of solar matter.
Engraved italics.
Her breasts weep.
Children in heaven
See us in splendor.
A stylized encounter.
Silky pubic hairs
Perineum digression
Each swallows a message.
Hades is just a carnival.
Then the umbilical surrender,
The mingled persona split.
Raptured admittance.
Modern painting.
Modern ambrosia.

Photograph by German photographer Susanne Kreuschmer --
www.susanne-kreuschmer.de, make –up Katrine Jakobsen –
model Patrizia Balcer (Facebook Patrizia Fotomodel)

Lovely girl.
White skin.
Blue eyes.
Tall and nubile.
Gun in hand.
Memories in vain.
Degenerate revolution.
One bullet then another.
Robins courting jaybirds.
Mystical courtesans.
Madness,
Both today and tomorrow.
The dignity of blood.
An enigma from death.
Her mouth opening.

Missing indifference.
Missing assumptions.

On my knees,
Crying again,
Dancing between extremes,
Interpreting departure,
Illustrating myself
From imagination.
A creation from limbo.
Never alive, but
Always on the verge.
She needs an outline,
Grateful for envisioning truth
Undressing in maliciousness.
Happiness never quite aligned.
Long ago in the bowels of beginning,
I disapproved of myself.
She: the passageway of all desire.
Wondering why.
Wondering who.

Reminded of good-bye.
A chessboard opens.
I checkmate quickly.
On the floor,
Swords etch
Moral questions
While flames consume me.
You with a lover
At each orifice.
Inaugurated after the protests,
The artists insist
On using redundant colors.
Ships carry away circumstances.
Alone and between words, I find that

Exaggerations consume my soul.
Real or absurdly desired,
Scenes of you remain.
Dangerous affirmations.
Dangerous provocations.

The collective is
Realized with imperfections.
Callous doctrines
Without reflection.
Only poets disclose.
I wander in awareness,
Understanding Van Gogh.
A symmetrical reshaping
Mimics breasts from heaven.
Fools establish contact
With unconscious desire,
Yet you outwit the gods.
Lying on your back, your
Legs spread openly
As the line advances
To see us in our casket.
Eternally buoyant in thought.
However, you never existed.
Utilize suggestion.
Utilize defeat.

Cowards betray the lonely.
The sea is your body.
Floating above is your face.
Painters penetrate women.
I reject existence.
Living where the damsels hide,
Deep in the impressions,
We guard the underside
Of not quite knowing.

Dreams filter provocateurs.
You slip into my character, from
Where we cannot find them.
They deny we are one.
The glory of myth.
Dangerous drama seeps
From saintly jealousy
Instigated by your beauty.
Intimidated, I remain outside.
Provoked, you erase my pretentions.
Unrefined meanings.
Unrefined coincidences.

Yesterday,
The precise ellipse
Established the language.
I resolved to have you.
Caged moments
Revered by spectators
Empty into circles.
Rhetoric landscapes
Welcome the naked.
You the object.
I the consequence.
At your nipples,
I apply myself,
Coiling my tongue.
The execution takes place.
Interior melancholy
Relents, becoming outward despair.
Out of love in a mirror,
You find your twin
Entwined with intrigue.
Precious austerity.
Precious ambiguity.

The Serpent
Knows his disagreement
With the world
On trial.
Pectoral differences.
Hiss and spit poison.
No valid reason for humankind.
Your remark about achievement.
Shapeless masses experiment.
Only genitals remain.
Qualifying for Christian piety,
I am alone
Inside your mind,
Among my thoughts
While making love
To the whores
I have known at sea.
They reject reality,
Gazing dreamily at the archangel.
A sane interpretation,
Knowing Ulalume is entombed.
Aesthetic possibilities.
Aesthetic modernity.

No premeditation,
Only rogue lashings
Cascading upon me.
Writhing
From the love
Denied.
Thorns cruising
In my bloodstream.
Quarantined
In homage.
Determining
Why the applause

And arrows
Culminate in my being.
Looking for collaborators
Outside my Dadaist thoughts.
Numbers in circles
Mean nothing.
Cannot be revived.
Lariat tightening.
You standing over me,
Not existing in reality,
Preceding surprise,
Preceding inspiration.

Certainly not.
The voices rediscover
Reactionary dualism.
Murky thoughts.
The eternal inhabitant
Identifies cancerous Medusa
As the lover I need.
Pantheistic demagogy.
The stitches holding me,
But not my mind.
I am inspired
By the eternal self-hatred,
Unbounded loathing.
Pain without clemency
A burdensome legacy.
You reading poetry,
Painting with a dagger.
Under my skin,
Your disease is
Purposely inflicted
For heaven's appreciation.
Beauty, more sexual than being,
Elevates me in chains.

Forget protesting.
Forget knowing.

The bar was closing.
I stood alone
She removed her top
You fell to your knees
I was asked to follow
In September rain
At the whipping post
Where achievement
Is perceived.
I cried during baptism.
They cried for a culprit.
The pain
Brought visionaries
With piercing eyes
To accuse voyagers.
My wounds opened
Your nipples dripping
Blood from my crime.
They pout
And accuse me.
Nothing is misunderstood
Parasites
Infest my mind
As your lovers
Shout
Folie de grandeur.

Cast that spell
Freeing us from doubt.
Thousands of years
Encased in guilt,
Rejecting poetry
Written for lovers.

I exit your womb

Bounding creativity.

Ulysses is on the phone.

With Penelope,

Mad with passion.

Paintings on the walls come alive.

Debauchery, not chivalry, was woken.

You simply said, "Last chance."

Judgment

Followed by the Ten of Swords.

Game over.

Leave your heart.

Take your mind.

Ulysses smiles at me.

"Are you a singular subject or a plural predicate?"

When I turn, I see

You naked

Running

Into the arms of Achilles.

Choose love.

Choose death.

WHEN THE AXIS RUNS PARALLEL TO THE OBTUSE THOUGHTS I HAVE, PERPENDICULAR TO THE MELODY I AM HEARING

Midnight.
The counterbalance
Of her undressing.
Nakedness overwhelms
The urges
For anything but raw,
Limitless entanglement.
I love her breasts.
I stop and smell that area,
Which elicits a smile
From every wanton
Dream maker.
I cannot get her close enough.
Step into me.
Crawl about.
Find me.
Flow through me.
Emote,
Glorious you.
Touch.
Just amorous
Expressions
Satisfy us.
Transcend boundaries.
Become me,
And I, you.
Us—an instant,
A connection,

Photograph by Scottish photographer Stuart McAllister

Unyielding,
Unknown,
Unequalled.
Paired consciousness
Bound
By pleasure,
Circling poetically.
A symphony,
Neither
You nor I.
We the abstract.
We the amorphous.
We the ambiguous.
Countenance.
A collective of love.
Suddenly,
A melody
From a Haydn string quartet
Wraps around us,
Shaking me from you.
I float away
To that instant
Before thought.
Through
Cézanne,
Renoir,
Monet,
And
Van Gogh, I arrive
At Gauguin.
I find myself
In Tahiti.
The pain from his
Tortured mind
Drives me further.
Now I am

Photograph of American Model/Artist Chantel Bacon

Lying on a bed
With Munch's dying sister.
I the palette
Washed with color.
Ornette Coleman
Pushes me into
Dissonance.
Contacting,
Contracting,
Sifting
Through
Chaos.
Beyond Faulkner.
Saxophones
And
Trumpets.
Gauges and wires.
Timeless clocks
Out of date.
In the clear
Moonlight,
Clouds
Touch us.
Glorious
Choirs,
Naked angels,
Surround me.
Magic carpet
Clergymen
Paint
Confessional panels
Opposite
From tomorrow.
Charlie Christian
Waves good-bye,
Awakening duality,

Mesmerizing the patio
Debutantes.
Mozart and I
Chase women.
The jungle music
Hits the mainstream.
White people
In bomb shelters.
A thousand steps
Past the years,
I return on
The tram
From the heavens.
A messenger,
Now amused
With the moment and
In conflict,
Drills for gold,
Just one of my favorite things.
Skeptical of my landing,
Lewis Carroll invites
Alice and Gisèle Prassinos
To work the back room,
With all
The Madonna's painted
By surrealists
Now in the colander,
Sifting out the ethereal.
Beautiful nymphs
Wake Nureyev.
I stretch my legs,
Transforming eternity.
I am melody.
I am grace.
I am the faun
Traveling

Artwork by Spanish artist Modesto Roldan

Through reams of treasured art
To arrive on stage,
Desiring
The essence of all.
Passion acts.
No director,
Just me,
Naked and unafraid.
I am the culmination,
The chosen one to move farther,
The aggressor with creativity.
I am a close-up
Without a shadow,
Ethereal, an ideal,
Pure thought,
Pure philosophy,
Pure art.
Purity awaiting
Hedonism.
Back to being invisible,
To Brazil.
Gilberto and Getz.
The wave
With
Sinatra and Jobim.
I want to make love
To the
Girl from Ipanema.
Colored girls from Bahia
Dress me
In what
The eyes of a woman
Find attractive.
John Coltrane
Pushes past
Space

While
Steel mills spew
Into the lake.
I am empty space,
Between perfection and genius.
John Kennedy appears in a Corvette.
Bob Dylan is driving.
I follow them.
The liquid in stemware
Never empties.
Who am I?
Spirituality
Is no atonement
For sketches
Displaying what is
Apparent.
I am in Notre Dame Cathedral
With Guinevere.
St. Genevieve
Arranged for the nuns
To lend us a room.
Soon, Catherine the Great
Meets us.
In Rome,
We make love
Blessed by Athena.
Caesar greets us,
Thinking I am Margaret Atwood.
Black coffee.
Alternate phrasing.
Metaphysical surroundings.
The Devil and the goddess
Approach.
That is when it happens:
Spears at dawn.
This practice run

Photograph by Italian photographer Mariano
Annoni – model & artist Giancarla Parisi

Is ending.
The fragmented fall.
I am
Entwined tight.
My seduction
Appears
Without being,
Lingering
Over me,
Listening for reactions.
My fingers hit the keys.
"Summertime" plays.
Full sexuality.
Speeding forward,
Past
Pollock,
Past
Fellini,
Through
Meet the Beatles.
Revolver, and
Sergeant Pepper.
Running through
"Jungles of Vietnam,"
"Let It Bleed."
Pavarotti
Singing "Ave Maria,"
Finally beyond
"Early Morning Rain."
From my youth,
That murky distance
Of turmoil and lovemaking.
I see what can never
Be seen by the young:
A blindness,
A straddling,

Artwork by French artist Audrey Marienkoff

A compromise.
The angel Gabriel
Comes to us all
With an announcement
To live joyously.
Perfectly fading
From a short instrumental,
I am aware.
There she is
Across from me,
Buoyant,
Conniving.
Yet I am the cad.
Queen-to-knight
Checkmate.
The white pieces brood,
Not understanding
Archetypes as architects
Designing heaven.
In a circular motion,
I fall to my knees,
Weeping for my mother.
Then, like
A silky curtain gently flowing,
I hear a voice,
Your voice,
As you become me.
Twine securing
When I reach
For you.
The honey-colored
Distance
That separates
Every thought
From the others
Collides with happiness

I once felt.
Your beautiful face
In cabaret lighting.
Your body
Bathed in
My memories.
I existed
Just for us,
To love
And be loved,
Knowing the more one loves,
The less of one
There is to love.
Yet Brutus
Called me
Ambitious.
Skeletal remains
Are found in catacombs,
The tinderbox,
Where delinquency
Teaches
Harbormasters
A lighthouse
Has more to teach them
Than the Coliseum.
I whine.
I search for you.
I see you staggering.
No, that is I,
Broad-shouldered,
Conditioned to believe,
Willing to gamble,
Fated to lose.
Captain Robert Walton
Saw my battered alter ego,
A body searching for meaning,

Photograph by Scottish photographer
Stuart McAllister-model Emma Rutherford

Never noticing me
Within,
Where
My lovers now
Weep for me.

God, with a smile
On her face,
Taps
Me on the shoulder.
In a mist
Holy and sane,
Unearthly but whole,
She offers her breasts,
Large and warm.
Then she offers more,
So I deny
Earthliness,
Already knowing that
What must be is
Rippling,
Coalescing,
Dispersing,
Nocturnally disappearing
Inside lyrical passion,
Painting me
On grotesque
Intellectual canvases
With
Diabolical angels
And
Tortured souls.
Then,
Then,
During a deep kiss
Deeper than regret,

Photograph by Scottish photographer Stuart McAllister

More pungent
Than naked shame,
A Holy Spirit
Whispers,
"From antiquity,
There have been women poets. The smell
Of their wombs
Will always
Be sweeter than man's fortune."
I thought of all
The lovely legs
I have been between
From then until now.
And tomorrow.
And tomorrow.

Artwork by Russian/Italian artist Tomaeva-Gabellini Fatima

Couplet Breaks—Corruption, Anarchy, or Just the Opposite

Written with L. Thomson

I collide
With conspirators.
Gossamer wings enfold me,
Swirling hues of pastel.
Reminiscences
In translucent opalescence.
Liquid on the precipice.
A devious pleasure,
Flirting with Pandora's box.
A sharp, metallic vibrancy
Aggravates the climax.
Mythical marauders,
Malingering without regard for me,
Infect my thoughts,
Cautioning me in my sleep amid my
Coquettish dreams
Of masquerading angels
Prowling cathedral spires,
Ethereally watchful
After our tragedy.
Turbulence startles me.
The palette turns stormy:
Tranquility transformed.
Rough edges—prickly thorns—

*Photograph by German photographer
Jasmina Sun – model Patrizia Balcer
(Facebook Patrizia Fotomodel)*

Piercing,
Drawing blood,
Warm blood,
Rich, red blood.
My lover's watchful eye
Follows the drips,
Then the flow.
How it gathers,
Gathers,
On cold, white titles.
Tonight,
A martyr comforts
Another lamented heroine.
Curled up amid divine images,
I am betrayed, my
Fraudulence revealed,
Nakedly exposed:
A labyrinth leading to
Ravenous but empty
Orgasms.
Circling and cackling, I am
Held in a patina of fear, on the
Jackals' trail.
They have my scent, those
Frenzied scavengers
Ripping flesh from bones,
Thoughts from imagination, and
Waking my being.

Savoring the moment,
Delicious and audacious,
I am my delight.
A gunsmith with my flesh
Emboldened and brazen
I peer into the now.

Photograph by German photographer
Jasmina Sun – model Patrizia Balcer
(Facebook Patrizia Fotomodel)

I peer into my reflection
From a million
Distorted mirrors.
You claim your innocence.
I return your gaze.
The maze taunts
Escapees from the past,
Prisoners in spaced interludes.
Under this stream of consciousness,
Body and spirit part ways,
Prone to confusion.
Reabsorbing into ourselves, we
Claim the other exists
When the turmoil intoxicates us.
Fallen from heaven and
Caught by Franceschini,
I can feel you,
Feel you,
Grouping, fidgeting, panting,
Avoiding all intolerance.
My fingers find your stigmata.
Your cranial sutures unravel.
An autopsy in disrepair.
Lack luster in comparison to a mad man's sighs
Lingering death paints erratically.

Photograph by German photographer
Jasmina Sun – model Patrizia Balcer
(Facebook Patrizia Fotomodel)

Uneasy worshippers,
Anomalies in torture chambers,
Turn to me.
An absent melody is
Sensed, not heard;
On the verge;
Captured, but never held;
Apathetic about rescripting
Except
When illusions
Liquefy,
Leaving me
Wickedly unclothed,
Pure and ideal,
Open.
Another artist
Attempts to imagine
My backside.
His face
Is drenched in the sweat
From my breast

SPITTOON POPSICLES

The clinic was cold.
The room was cold.
The table was cold.
The injection was cold.

You are blonde.
Your breasts are soft,
Large, and firm.
You lean over me.
      I inhale your breath.
Mints and champagne come to mind.
      I want to kiss you.
      I want to undress you.
      I want to bury myself in you.
      I watch the surgical instruments.
      I anticipate my awakening.
The deep, fine line from the scalpel blade
Crosses my chest.
Blood starts to appear.
A Joni Mitchell song plays in my head,
Or maybe it is a Judy Collins tune.
      I wanted to make love to both of them.
      I have always wanted them.
      I have always wanted,
But those clouds,
Those apparitions,
Those psychotic ballet dancers in my head
With knives and forks
Poking around in abandonment—
They make circles within calendar numbers,
Bending the alphabet to suit the images,

Photograph by Scottish photographer
Stuart McAllister – model Sarah Mua

Images in bold colors,
Images in mad, horrific scenes,
Images unknown to any other images.

      I feel your hand moving inside my chest,
Warm blood anticipating every escape.
There are no IVs,
Just us.
Just me.
When you suggested murder,
The excitement rose inside me.
Turning off my indifference and
Spinning in tangos made of lies,
You have found my heart.
Those scissors are thought-provoking.
You are lovely in white and cinnamon.
Pouting lips and wide eyes.
Your skirt drops to the floor,
Into the blood ever collecting.
Moving away from me, you begin to spread
The space between your legs, spilling your blood
My hand opens your body cavity.
Poisonous snakes, roaches, and hyenas rush out,
Poised with historical ambition,
Numbing their commitment to hunt and kill.
They, like me, are crazed with hunger.
Cages made of flesh appear as I remember
Fists pummeling all imagination.
Gossamer ideas stumble from Homer's paragraphs.
      I am being either killed or reborn once more.

You were skinning me of all reverence.
Then you remembered there was nothing to remember.
The room vacillates from incorrigible to dismissive.
Your knees shake from the orgasm.
You come closer and kiss my lips,

Forgetting that madness is perpetual motion.
You straddle my face
Closer
And tighter,
Suffocating me.
Racing to surpass "The Rocking-Horse Winner,"
          I am aloft,
Being swallowed by you,
By you, in you—as you.

Trumpets sound.
Trumpets sound.
The crowd rises up in applause.
The games in the arena are to begin.

A perfect autumn Sunday with Indian summer weather,
Cadillacs making the circle with prom queens waving.
Penises and breasts on grills billowing mesquite smoke flavoring.
In the pit, the immigrant boys wrap razor wire around me.
"Start it up," I hear over the sound system.
Dignitaries bow and shake hands with fund-raisers.
Kids buy the baby mammals they will toss into the ring.
The raging buffalos are doped with amphetamines.
The wild herd is set loose.
Good bloody beginnings, excellent applause—around and around,
Death churns indifference into oblivion.

Is that you I see?
Now, in another place through time,
The black boys wrap me in thick rubber,
With neon paint, gasoline, and nails carefully placed inside.
It's the first real run of the new season.
Racecars are adorned with the logos of voyages.
          I see beautiful young women in little more than bewildered wantonness.
Prayers are announced over the loud speaker, asking Jesus for action.
Shredded human parts in spicy sauces are ready for sale.

Teenagers are given fiery slingshots to boost the excitement.
The combat drivers, some pointed in the opposite direction, hit the gas pedals hard.
Some say it is the impact that hurts the most. I believe it is the desertion.

> GUINEVERE: Sir Lionel!
> "Do you recall the other night when I distinctly said you might
> Serve as my escort at the next town fair?"*

The midway is electric with lights and attention-catching noises.
Promiscuous young lovers and families are alive with anticipation.
The daring rides, lingering cooking oils, sticky candy, and abundant laughter.
There are arched entrances where exits never existed.
> I am at the games, the gunshots ringing, the pinballs rattling, the balloons
> bursting.
Put a coin on a number. When the guillotine comes down,
My head will bounce and roll into a hole. You will win
Not some intellectual fantasy, but brute force.
There is no future, but this moment lasts until thought prevails.
We all celebrate death, that magical part of life that surprises everyone.
Choo-choo, chug-chug—the trains descend to the lower levels,
Where knowledge is buried behind product placement.
Utility electrodes are connected to every skull.
Colors only imagined in wasteland horizons.
The drugs dispersed and the mind monitored.
Sex alongside cars in alcoves. Unpleasant consequences.
Red Nipples and bullets—well-handled machine guns.
Demigod admirals recite a medley of mental disorders.
> I still love you as a jaded antique varnish collapses outside of me,
With hacksaws and power drills making my decisions.
Diamond-shaped hearts like acid crystals dispense jokers.
> I see my ambitions in coarse halos around God-forbidden anarchy.
Hard, recollection-loaded pistols of forgiveness fire incessantly.

"Tutti frutti au rutti.

---

* Alan Jay Lerner, *Camelot* (New York: Random House, 1961).

Tutti frutti au rutti.
Tutti frutti au rutti.
A-bop-bop-a-loom-op a-lop-bop-boom."*

       I have lost
All connection to the stained-glass mirror insistences that accompany a crashing dream
Taking place inside the turbulence, inside the derailment, inside the nightmare, inside the
outside reality, inside my cataclysmic thoughts,
Where the characters become feelings without expression in another alien landscape.
       I remember
That night
We met
Without you
Ever
Being there.
It
Was just me,
Just me,
Cold and on fire,
Cold and shivering,
Cold and alone,
Alone and without remembrance,
Contemplating the
Vanishing parodies
Clawing their way
Through my mind,
Out of my mind,
Into my mind.
Seeing you.
       I recall the view.

---

* Tutti Frutti - written by PENNIMAN, RICHARD / LABOSTRIE, DOROTHY / LUBIN, JOE

Artwork by Russian/Italian artist Tomaeva-Gabellini Fatima

DIVINITY IN QUESTION

The country girl
    By the seaside.
        My love embraces
The altitude
    Beyond the trueness
        Of deliverance.
I remember the waves rushing to the shore,
    Knowing omissions of speech,
        How the differences
Foretold what is to be.
    My lips trembling.
        Yours timid but moist.
The rapture
    And the summoning
        For foundations
Embedded in pious
    Puzzle pieces.
        On my knees,
Exercising the right
    To ask questions.
        My arms around your waist.
Intelligent, sentimental smiling.
    Ignoring moments,
        Watching the glare,
Underestimating the unknown,
    Anticipating separation.
        Breasts out,
Legs spreading.
    Your head on a blanket.
        The picnic basket.
Friendly dogs playing.
    The apple falls,

Sealing the deal.
The thought of your
     Simmering instincts.
         A mild surf laps at the shore.
Clouds mimic a symphony.
     Emotions insist that
         We taste again
Our favorite essence.
     Mining unknown activities
         As I search your mind.
Just a pinch of craziness.
     You perceive
         Devils deliberating,
The angels' runway
     Expanding in my mind,
         Swallows soaring,
Marco Polo on a journey.
     Your eyes undressing my face.
         Rippling anticipation.
That night in bed,
     Crippling fears,
         Voluntary hallucinations.
Finally alone,
     Naked, and warm.
         Breathing only accolades
Against the world's indifference.
     Your body on mine.
     My body on you.

Artwork by Russian/Italian artist Tomaeva-Gabellini Fatima

It was I.
     Was it you?
     Torrents welcoming hedonism.
Repetitious cat meows
     Encompassing our reverie.
     The newspaper arrives,
Reviews the encounter.
     Two frightened children under a blanket.
     The Sound of Music our background.

Forever platitudes.
  Believing in romantic,
    Par-excellence expressions.
Reflecting images of sin.
  No dark secrets are bleachable.
    When comparisons violate illustrations,
The three witches recite Poe.
  Philip of Macedonia
    Requests soothsayers
As Alexander conspires with gods.
  Fortune and love separate.
    Agreeable confrontations
Alleviative questions of forgiveness.
  I have two revolvers.
    The first to die is the liar.
Love is always expendable.
  Laughter ravishes the circumstance.
    Hamlet sourly approaches.
He hands me red wine,
  Holds a mirror to my face.
    Behind the image, he asks,
"Have you ever been loved?"
  Tears fill my eyes.
    Firing a shot to warn the artists,
Lady Macbeth undresses Lady Chatterley.
  Oedipus understands why
    The building erupts into fire.
We remain staring at each other,
  Neither demanding anything from the other.
    You passionate;
Me insane.
  I ask if cherubs are links
    Between
Impressionism and expressionism.
  You smile and fire
    The bullet drills into me.
Is there a difference between

Dimension and apparitions?
        You smile and fire again,
Telling me about incomprehensible love.
        The third shot opens my chest.
                Expansiveness awakens.
Standing, you remove your clothes.
        I try to stand, but another bullet hits me,
                Pushing me into a wall.
As I lie dying, you squat over me,
        Dig your fingers in my façade,
                And empty the gun.
Your love explodes,
        Nurturing deep hatred and
                Torching souls,
Souls that always lack,
        Souls that always miscarry.
                In lives never fulfilled
Penetrating the psyche.
        Introspecting on dismemberment,
                I see the creational expletives
Unraveling your superficial temperament.
        Saxophones speak to thoughts.
                Christian choirs notice I have value.
Nails appearing;
        Nails imbedding;
                Nails unforgiving.
I am devoured,
        Eagerly plagiarized.
                The third act will begin
Before the first.
        Epilogues include sacrificial assumptions.
                Witnesses at the end
Confess it was suicide.
        Operatic in stature,
                I say I had no idea

Puccini supplied the characters.
　　My body is doused
　　　　Chanel's Antaeus pour homme.
The tall, beautiful, blonde
　　With sinful breasts
　　　　Turns to literary sources,
Friday night references
　　Clubs and cabarets.
　　　　She undresses before her memory,
Her hand where my head would lie.
　　Owning nothing, she harmonizes
　　　　With reality.
A little girl with porcelain skin
　　Looks into the coffin.
　　　　Wearing a smile,
She kisses my check.
　　Tears drip on satin.
　　　　Peter Pan has been released
To orbit planets.
　　The mental attacks
　　　　Subside.
The intervention of pleasure,
　　Cockiness, and intelligence
　　　　Rests away.
A second image is portrayed.
　　Those who know
　　　　Laugh at the outrage.
There was only one.
　　My body is blessed,
　　　　Sent to hell.
I am in this place
　　Not that place,
　　　　A place in a place
Wondering,
　　Wondering why
　　　　We wonder,

Why Images never
    Leave a dream.
        Leave a dream

Photograph of French Model/Artist She nandoah

ANTICIPATION AND THE WRATH OF KNOWING

Bob Dylan sang,
"He not busy being born is busy dying."
Debussy ran to Rouen Cathedral,
Knowing that Monet was becoming.

I ask you to come closer.
I ask you to come closer.
I see you have a gun.
I see you have a gun.

The reflection in the mirror is perpetual.
The mirror hangs from a thread of thought
Conceived for forever.
Alice knows.

Afghan War

Shakespeare wrote,
"Out, out, brief candle!"
Beethoven played for Marie Antoinette,
Knowing that Mozart was extinguished.

I see you have a gun.
I see you have a gun.
I ask you to come closer.
I ask you to come closer.

The reflection in the mirror is transitive.
The mirror hangs from a thought on a thread.
It was conceived for pleasure.
Constance Chatterley knows.

Gulf War

Ibsen wrote,
"You have never loved me. You have only thought it pleasant to be in love with me."
Dizzy looked at the barriers,
Knowing that Miles was fearless.

I ask you to come closer.
I see you have a gun.
I ask you to come closer.
I see you have a gun.

The reflection in the mirror is unconscious.
The mirror hangs from a thought thread
Conceived for examination.
Hester Prynne knows.

Vietnam War

Camus wrote,
"Mother died today. Or maybe yesterday. I can't be sure."
Ulysses went to sea,
Knowing that Achilles was pretentious.

I see you have a gun.
I ask you to come closer.
I ask you to come closer.
I see you have a gun.

The reflection in the mirror is premature.
The mirror hangs from a thread thought
Conceived for immortality.
Anna Karenina knows.

Korean War

George Sand wrote,
"The world will know and understand me someday."
Judas counted his silver,
Knowing that Jesus was a gambler.

I ask you to come closer.
I see you have a gun.
I see you have a gun.
I ask you to come closer.

The reflection in the mirror is premature.
The mirror hangs from a thread thought
Conceived for immortality.
Sylvia Plath knows.

World War II

Conan Doyle wrote,
"Mediocrity knows nothing higher than itself, but talent instantly recognizes genius."
Washington counting his slaves,
Knowing that Jefferson was theorizing.

I see you have a gun.
I ask you to come closer.
I ask you to come closer.
I see you have a gun.

The reflection in the mirror is premature.
The mirror hangs from a thread thought
Conceived for immortality.
Anastasia Nikolaevna knows.

World War I

In confession: "Bless me Father, for I have sinned."

At the time, I just did not understand
It was the last century.
Philosophers were intellectual evangelists.
All artists were mad.
Music was profound.
Poets skewered themselves.
Painters transformed light.
Men were cruel;
Women, vessels;
Children, unwanted;
Animals, tortured.
The world abandons itself.
Yesterday is today;
Tomorrow, a funnel.
I liken myself to death.
Everything I touch meets God.

At the altar, I perform my penance: to speak with God.

I can come closer.
Aim your gun.
You can come closer.
Guernica. The Third of May, 1808.

THE SEA NEVER DECEIVES YOU WHEN YOU ARE DREAMING

I knew the sun had risen without any coherence. It resembled the rich yellow fields of Van Gogh.
My mind, incurring portraits of every artist's future, sees all in absolute upheaval.
Knowing I am me for the first time, I baptize myself.

The weight lessens and the thought of me lingers in the minds of all my mistresses.
I search for all that is excessive, but I have gone far beyond what I am thinking.
This ascension leads to a striking nude in slashes and splashes of importance.

Within a dreamscape, all the heroes are bound, revered, and thrown into the sea.
A woman with her arms open sits on a flat rock, listening to the roar of waves.
Innocent to the smiles of her dead devotees, she is beholden to curious tides.

Is that you I see, one down strap revealing your breast? Minutes turn slowly.
Communion is served with pathos. Recipients are asked to interpret incompetence.
You arch your back to receive all glory, all honors.

Piano keys, flesh in my mouth, subsequent promises without direction.
I understand why incompleteness echoes to lovers who are empty of passion.
Dreams running wild cannot dissuade me that the storms will reach port.

A paintbrush colors the fringes as the center catches fire: tipped blue flames.
A sun filled with threadbare lies is arranged in flurries of expression.
I try to feel the difference, but amnesty is only until twilight.

An appointment is planned with trivial affirmations and moments of obsessive compassion.
Uncomfortable with my reasoning, you suggest solitary Russian roulette.
In my becoming what I seemed, your confinement encases my ill-starred wishes.

Never numbering my arrangements, the wind disperses all my recollections.
So two bodies fill the containers of each other, knowing that failure will be permanent,
I am lost again, exaggerated beyond the ascension path of another's thoughts.

Walking down the paths of grave sites I see that all bear my name.
　　You curtsy at my coffin. Your face next to mine, your lips mouthing my ideas.
　　　　Ordinary occurrences once dispelled now contort because of your hurried enticement.

The journey has begun. One step runs into the other till we are pebbles kicked from sanity.
　　Tall buildings crumble as planes sign autographs in the sky above them.
　　　　We recall the afternoon when weapons were hid under every liquor stain.

I hold you now in solitude, alone in the darkness, missing you as thoughts collide with refrains.
　　Failing disappointments contour into me; a cold, lifelong snake crawls about my heart.
　　　　The bulk of sordid admissions made of eternal slices holds me as I descend.

Impossible figures that reward love with death recollections triumph by my second drowning.
　　You at the center, painted in haste, are lost to my arms and never a romantic hero.
　　　　Our silence is a long passage down a dark, foreboding decline without an escape.

When will I find the path that exhales the sorcerer's rapture enfolding me as I journey to myself?
　　The rising, never-ending sea calls to every lonesome sailor lost in prophetic disappointment.
　　　　Court the disasters that turn men from tortured to impassioned yet always lost.

The crashing of the ships on the rocks. Sirens and mermaids breast-feeding misconceptions.
　　Now the tides bunk with the planets. Adrenaline thoughts are encrusted with enchantment.
　　　　Your smile is locked in my mind; your dagger digs deeper in my chest.

Overwhelmed by the madness of the seas, the lull brings thunder-inviting lightning.
　　Budging biceps, ropes, and superstitions of righteous warriors appear in endless succession.
　　　　Fascinated by waves obscuring the sunset, I long for you to seduce me.

Watery world seen through eyes blackened with tears shed over departures from abject drudgery.
　　Down we go into the cistern that grinds men to pulp and where nothing is accomplished.
　　　　Whipped with perfumed-laced beliefs, our quivering thoughts yearn for love again.

The storm continues. Dead men on board reflected in cracked mirrors forever reappearing.
　　Tied to the mast, I hear the shuffling of passersby who died millennia ago without sinning.
　　　　Walking on her hands, she, the most beautiful one, wraps her legs around my neck.

"How much pain can you endure?" she asks, announcing her presence with beguiling wit.

I'm writhing with impatience. My name takes flight as Hans Holbein paints my portrait.

I relive the moment while negating all the chandelier romances I once condemned.

Unseen and then seen, an ark unburdens its crew, allowing them to lament the passages of destruction

When I was young, I contemplated marbleized glass too fragile for imaginative understanding.

Now, as the wind strokes my chest, you ask me to repeat our vows—without any bloodletting this time.

Your large breasts pout, forcing the dazzling agony of being completely corrupt and scorning all faith.

Growing more luxuriant, your figure strains against the silky fabric that my mind inhabits.

You painfully remove my eyes, putting them in a locket you toss out to sea.

I cannot know if "do not" means the same as "come forward," so I dream all possibilities.

On the deck, I have you in every blue midnight star's obituary, icy-cold and perfect.

Life has lost its touch; thus, I am astray, with nothing in waiting or moving toward me.

With gravest insanity, we uniquely communicate with targets flowered for our fantasy.

A shot across the bow personifies the agony between two souls and condemns our voyage.

As promised, your body is punctured and impregnated with diamonds and numbness.

I see through you, the vulgar nature of corruption—the hangman's noose and a keelhauling.

Witnessing the unamicable, I steep in deep suffering as a halo drifts away from Mary.

A crowd of mad sailors, demoralized by self-conception, shout, "Kill this poet."

In a paranoiac embrace, we encounter the saints, who swap you amid their crass exclamations.

Your activities are repugnant to reality, so you stow away in the bridgework of fantasy.

Kisses between your legs seem natural. Unanswered solutions inspire ideas.

Strangers gather around fools, so I invite my mind to have a drink with my conscience.

Love is lost and futile. All this mental anguish against a soul bleached with gossamer memories.

There you are, the beautiful mistress of the seas, bathed in light and cursed by love.

Seeing waves with imaginary protectors, metaphysical archetypes escape in a mental flight.

I never find what I am after, but I know that hell will be a relief from the exorcism of life.

Crimes are committed in my name. The anarchists choose floating barges to explain art nouveau.

Treblinka footprints stomp us so deeply into self-regret that we forget the oblique journey continues.

Being human, not gods, leaves us open for measured hatred. Deluded, we submit easily.

Then the corroded razor blades and austere innuendoes sift us through our punishment.

I can feel the screws, for the hinges drill through me. How perfect being disciplined feels.

Love is not the pastime of amateurs. Those with ambition expect tears tinged with pure blood.

There is no sanctuary for my distorted mind inflamed with notions from an rebuked adolescence.

Cousins and relations connecting with the apparatus for misunderstanding climb into luxury.

I need you, but the ashes and the dust that assembled to reflect absence dream dire consequences.

No sweetheart salutes. Sleep-rendering diversions escape into anthologies of remorse.

The declarations ring from the spires: "I am dead. Come feast on the remains of my calamity."

How dare I exist as resolute when the gods desired obedience as I began to understand.

Traveling toward existence, I run from grudges and paw your renditions of my guilt.

Rare thoughts scourge the precipices inside my mind, seeking observations of commitment to security.

The ocean rules. The waves never hesitate to overwhelm the boldness that counterfeits desire.

My eyes see myself tossed on the fiery waves without fearing the apparitions—ever.

I plead with the guards outside your heart. They hated my smile, my background, and my bravado.

Slowly, you have me baptized. The pain is so overwhelming that my admissions suture our love forever.

Between the desperate and the loved, we awaken, saying our good-byes and agonizing over our self-mutilation.

Is it the sun or the Son?
      Oh my God,
            I comprehend the immensity.
               Oh my God.
Now, in this instant, I understand

What all art is saying.

With extraordinary quickness, I become *that* image.
Pending birth, I hold my cord, knowing I will be unencumbered by my existence.
Jesus and I watch Jesus and me on the cross, telling sailor stories about the voyages to come.

Photograph by Canadian photographer Bonita (Bonnie) Harris

THE STRANGER INSIDE

Cowardice
This current life
Cast off calendar
Shadow of days
My past
Wrapped
In miraculous saves
Bells toll
Crush mindful
Resurrections
I see me again
But in shadow
Arranging seasons
No guiding light
Following
The path to the sea
The ever distance
Forlorn yet soft
Always in motion

Like deceit
Like decay

Short black skirt
Blue eyes
Your breasts
Moist
From my tears
What war was I in?
I remember shame
As tears
Genuflected

Photograph by English photographer Warwick Upton

To paradoxes
Playing cards with lives
Consequences
Transforming
Kids to corpses
No matter
Justice is
Unconscious
Eyes blinded
By anticipation

Like evil
Like extraction

Sadness
Columns in rows
I loved your embrace
As styles
Changed
We grew apart
Reveries colliding
Indifferent to emotions
You wedded
I rode the train
That never stopped
Not even
To look back
In sorrow
I cling to night
For I am elusive
Entombed in thought
Arrogant
Blemished by experience

Like stillness
Like sin

Jealous incantations
For adventures
In silk beds
With talented
Linguistic masters
They flayed
Words that rhymed
With scores
Making narrow
Escapes
You on me
Then me on you
We were the moment
Haunted
By cultured reason
Those proper nouns
March
And verbs are called
To trample plagues

Photograph by English photographer Warwick Upton

Like Hate
Like Hysteria

In the dream
Within a dream
My Mother appears
I ask, "Am I in this dream"?
She asks, "Why"?
Because the distance
Is abstract and I am
No longer acting
The dream within a dream
Became The Dream

I was dreaming
Ethereally flawed
Except
For you
Captive in dreaming
At the periphery
The sting
From the bite
Never felt

Like Assassination
Like Abstention

The choreographers
Are dead
Bombs killed their
Visions
Now dancers
Faun for Poets
Though they too
Have lost their steps
I search for you
In the wasteland
In the menacing
Thoughts
My mind
Denies me
Performance
Philosophy
Without words
Only dramatists
Searching

Like Fortitude
Like Failure

The precipice
Crumbles
Decreasing
My time
I see the turbulence
The Ocean
Demanding
I dissect
The metaphor
From the allegories
Mist from waves
Caresses my flesh
Impersonating
Your tongue
Rehearsing
Insanity for a living
I fall again
From the cross
Into your arms

Like Stealing
Like Strangling

The sign
After death
Says, Welcome
I enter a room
Of mystery and mirrors
She appears
While every
Image of me
At every age
Parallels
Moments of time
All reflections

Form
An idealized me
Becoming her
She kisses my lips
"You are me"? I ask
She replies, "No,
I am you".

Like Noumenon
Like Nonsense

And I, again
Board the ship.

A Lost Eyelash Floating Out to Sea

Philip K. Dick used my brain for a while.
He and I were watching the tape recorder
Go round and round
When he pulled out his gun,
Brutus had just confessed to Sam Spade.
I was with Frank Lloyd Wright,
Contemplating the two L's in Lloyd.
When Tarzan swung to meet us,
The bullets came fast and flying.
Inconsistent with November 22, 1963,
Alfie counted the caskets from Afghanistan.
Grandchildren in giant mix masters,
Always and forever in cash-made dreams.
The beginnings of what we never thought
before.
Hippie accomplishments in war-torn
California.
Now you stand naked with sponge breasts.
God left the poker game when the money
from Viet Nam dried up.
From the ashes, Phoenix rose,
We slashed the for sale sign.
From the center, from the arc, from the wanting, from the blur,
And from a caustic me to a juvenile you.

Photograph by Scottish photographer Stuart McAllister

Geometric horizons in parallelogram departures
Curl into gossamer illusions torn from centric deviations.
Yet in surreal passages of quantum time, you still reflect.
Poignant asterisks from archipelago misunderstandings
Invite musk oxen to discuss the disappearance of intellectuals.
Kurtz, mad with sanity, reaches his hand out to John Paul Jones,
Releasing shredded circumferences as days stray from strangers,

Those intervals of perched eloquence donning togetherness.
Sympathetic tortoises wrap around your waist as sex begins.
In sin as in life, you laugh to keep me from understanding.
Basement sweethearts on pool tables pose naked for Murillo.
Blood easily oozes from my mouth as I lie in state once more.
Removing the brush from Magritte's hand, you solidified history.
Tubercular renegades pose as Confederate legends.
They dig deep graves to announce the release of Frankenstein's daughter.
I cannot remember when the rape stopped, but I do remember her wanting me,
The crew rubbed kerosene between her thighs to bless our fortune.
A Mount Olympus fortuneteller sliced the neck of a Picasso figure
Because you thought my blood and that of a predator would blend
From the center of the arc, from the wanting, from the blur,
And from Renaissance me to unveiled you.

Juan Ramón Jiménez wrote a beautiful, eight-line poem.
I ran a scalpel blade down my arms, thinking about the softness of my neck.
A playful girl with a perfect body asked for my money, then my love.
I shot her through the head and danced with her reflection in my mind.
We ran for the exits before you turned to face your disappearing self.
At the statue of Napoleon in Cherbourg, Morley Callaghan introduced me
To the informer, who was dressed in petticoats and engaged in sexual brig activity.
Still bleeding from my assassination, I looked for the French-Canadian damsel
Her hand caught the bullet dismissed by the cavalcade of theorists at Daly Plaza.
She was nursing an old, disabled vagabond sailor with cocaine and champagne.
There were telegraph secretions meowing alongside acquiescent futurists who were erasing science.
In the sublime decadence, one mind wept within the pages of a postwar Hamilton novel.
Stumbling to get away from the assassins, I sat between Caulfield and Raskolnikov.
Eye to eye, mind to mind, we stared and spoke of The Stranger, which would change us all.
The Maple Leafs were losing to the Canucks when the stripper approached our table.
She asked to be flayed, so Hemmingway undressed her. Gogol scooped up the remains.
On drugs but beyond knowing, I held you naked until my erection started speaking.
The doctors arrived; Zhivago opened my head and let out my thoughts.
He then drank with Jekyll, ready to hunt down Mary Jane Kelly and Patricia Krenwinkel
From the center of the arc, from the wanting, from the blur,

And from believing me to accepting you.

Kafka points to the clock and suggests we never trust bloodied undressed whores
We inject hormones and wait for mummification of the jezebels who are training to be nurses.
Paladin smells your scant panties, grows taller, and arm-wrestles Wild Bill.
I am alone, dealing cards to sewer rats that double down on every hand.
The arrow easily glides through my thoughts and carries me to a critique of reason.
Carrion, the language of yesterday's anti-destiny generation, hollows my soul.
Yet I drink. And you, yes, you count the lines until the ending, until my dismissal.
In the lighthouse without services, I dream of you in fishnets, on my face.
My tongue is wild at every opening you provide. Then, without warning, I taste my blood.
Smoky, single-malt Scotch runs from the bullet holes, but, like the monster, I prevail.
Once the tarantella begins, the Corleone family, like dishwater, disappear down the drain.
"You are Tied to Me, Starbuck" is on the radio, so I stick an anal probe into eternity.
At night, Cronkite with the Baja Marimba Band plays "Rambling Gambling Man."
I know I have little to lose, so I become female and retire to a room with Cary Grant.
Churchill is profound, stating that victory has an absent audience unless Kennedy is shot.
In the poolroom, American women speaking Creole undress in order to emit spectral nuances.
Under the sheets, I ask for your hand in marriage. You prefer that I swallow poisoned scissors.
Holding your double-D's, you smile for the camera as I piece together my personality.
Then the bomb explodes. Bob Dylan chews peppermint gum as Joni Mitchell smokes a Players,
From the center of the arc, from the wanting, from the blur,
And from loving me to believing you.

In the alley, the blonde barmaid promises me her address and a knife if I change my mind.
Madly in love, Esmeralda and Dulcinea, allow me to film their affair with Mallarmé.
Yeats, dissecting Paris encounters, cannot wait for me to be murdered after MLK.
When she is speaking with Sinatra, the veil falls off Eva Braun.
A compromise in the atmosphere cannot mean a change of mind, just cold lake-effect snow.
You, with legs spread, apply different-size glow tubes while you play war games with Circe and Calypso.

To tell the truth, I am I, alone in salvation's last burned-out hideaway for insane poets.

Your faux orgasms with fluttering eye lids and nails digging are a trick of alcoholic bipolar misfits.

Standard deviations stay out in the rain as runaway understandings enlarge thinking.

On the eclipse, conviction devours exploration, staring at the conjunctions that time releases.

All summer long, my mind and I prepare for Marx to expose nationalism.

Blind love, exponential in its reverse designation, negates your encumbrances.

Jung perceives to analyze forces that flow from an anonymous view,

You and I leave sensational anal sex to the realm of forensic reality.

Steinem, crying clouds, knows that my friends will stampede against any illogical reasons.

Leaving the scene where the wars exist only in memory, I recount my father's conquests.

Christianity rewrites history as we inhale the passing years abundant with fractured failures.

The woman who openly loved me remarried: a minimal achievement without any vital force.

I am in a back room with shades, turning my back on elemental morality and ignoring maturity

From the center of the arc, from the wanting, from the blur,

And from dismissing me to waiting you.

White inheritors buying the San Andreas Fault wonder when writing will become extinct.

Germane to the issue is the depravity of the answers without their misanthropic implications.

Colloquial collogues surfing in folic misunderstanding simplify the murders they commit.

On the outskirts on mental capacity, I still linger on the touch of your tongue on my genitals.

Missing universal understanding for my rival thoughts, suicide attempts seem rational.

When Christ leaves Judaism he decides to pepper spray his followers and go into politics.

My insanity was evolving into melancholy when you approached with harmonic indifference.

While I am on the mend, the priests anchor me to the idealists in my mind, who always misunderstand.

Poe told me that the Raven's "nevermore" immersed his ruptured mind in Baudelaire's mistakes.

The prisoner who lives in my mind (outside heaven) drinks the blood of pacifists who betrayed him.

This audience waits for an encore, so I undress and become the faun in Carmen's dark passion.

As I am walking on water, the drugs pulsate and I begin to understand Nietzsche.

Commodore Perry, with his zipper open, locks doors and demands his ego back.

Beckett and Chekhov find me in a stateroom, chained to the bulkhead of materialistic confusion.

Egalitarian revolutionaries debate decision makers in true time, referring to tomorrow in the past tense.

Tethered contrasts chastise storms. The horizon individualizes and forces the links between ideas.

I courted you at the Basilica, where statues defended our nakedness by dismissing all modern approaches.

Lorca and Neruda, playing dice with fortune and poverty, know that words sleep in dreaming minds.

The Threepenny Opera becomes a for-flushers process of doubt, a precursor to finite bad-luck images

From the center of the arc, from the wanting, from the blur,

And from sacrificing me to justifying you.

The increased importance of sublime interferences compels the exorcist to wrestle with dominance.

Circumspect and circumcised, Asian consecrators question the meaningless as acceptable choices.

Listening to Delius, I find that universal reason unravels the swinging sunshine by way of Emerson's principles.

I cannot burden myself with the truth when our significance borrows comprehension from simplicity.

Cultural imperatives hunt me down for my plain thought, for my demanding sympathy for those who are in need.

Juliet of the Spirits and I are in bed with John and Yoko, our performance based on the receipts from minstrel shows.

Those who smile and ride pregnant mules from the Promised Land refuse to recognize chaos from faith.

Never giving way to reality, the clueless courts stand alongside ubiquity, denying unrestrained ideas.

The destruction of artistic sentiment encourages Samson and those who had been forgiven to kill once more.

Supporting myself on the verge of the edge, I watch you have sex openly with the church hierarchy.

Our cosmos, swilling its outcomes in my mind, witnesses God's glory-stars on fire—dying again.

On the corner, junkies drink nitroglycerin and condemn the alphabet for having letters.

The philosophy of psychology drips murderously from liquid irony as purpose stands against time.

Being a crusader, I killed for riches and raped for love, inseminating justice with the semen of fertile social reptiles.

Augustine never thought the main event would bring superstitious freedom to prism federalists.

Knowing me, Greek tragedians defend you because your sexual misconduct is revolutionary for abstraction in art.

Suicide bombers, the new-wave painters of life, splatter into a contrariness of visual rods and cones.

On the docks, you spread your legs. The lice appear as ratchets, looking for heads to twist.

Leading me through hell, you point out all the comforts of continual pain continuing being painful

From the center of the arc, from the wanting, from the blur,

And from eliminating me to worshipping you.

Photograph by Scottish photographer Stuart McAllister – model Emma Rutherford

ACCOLADES FROM THE ANGELS IN HEAVEN WHOSE MINDS HAVE BIRTHMARKS

I should be dead
I should be dead
I should be dead
I should be dead
I should be dead
I should be dead
I should be dead
I should be dead
I should be dead
I should be dead
I should be dead
I should be dead
I should be dead

Most of all, I love you so.
Most of all, I love you so.
Most of all, I love you so.

Art Blakey plays that mood-indigo excellence that permeates a knowing crowd.
Quarantined in the cellophane menagerie,
I leave the room to check my mind.
The drums address my rolling thoughts.
There is always a master of ceremonies.
I call myself to the stage,
Achilles and I, Ulysses and I.

Pieces of silver—the cordial invitation that has centered human thinking.
Adriatic passengers ask for sobriety identification.
From the lower deck, I spot a redhead.
Indulgently, I snicker as I stare.
"Paris used to be Berlin," I tell her.

She removes her panty hose.

Confinement has conceived a cerebral character from fiction.
She asks if I have money.
She asks if I have drugs.
She asks if I have power.

Her father owns all the snake pits in the world, including the ones in our nightmares.
I tell her I have a mind and the world does not exist outside it.
The waves hug the ship. The white foam atop—a final way to say good-bye.
In her cabin, she strips and gets on her knees.
I smell the dignity of orbs enchanted by nothingness.
I feel the rolling and subtle nuances of oceanic commotion.
My internal loneliness makes this scene tolerable.
I touch her hair and guide her head into the safety of my chest,
Or so
I imagine.
She and I at the altar. Yes, I do.
Yes, she does.
The best man takes my place,
Dancing through the cracks in this orbit.
Humankind's ugliness disappears as lush gardens unveil themselves.
It is just the liquor.
It is my turn to return the obligatory favor.
At the bar, I find an unpetaled flower.
I just swallow her whole, without regard.
I have stolen her, ingested her, relished her.
Now
I am alone in the room,
In the asylum,
Asking myself,
Can I love?
Can I feel?
Am I?
The train stops. Most of the passengers disembark.
I think I am heading to Russia with Lenin

Or
Riding the Orient Express while in bed with Agatha Christie.
Either way, I am absent from any reality.
While I am playing twenty-one, the cards are blank
My silhouette, my shadow, and me,
An amateur in a wordless play
On the runway, a bus stops to take me to the airport.
We had crashed into the achievements of humanity.
All are expected to row.
We all have to pay.
I tell the angels of my ambitions
In decimals,
The minus effect of everlasting love.
They take my face in their hands and weep.
I leave the cause of my misery,
Noticing the mansions of overcast instability.
My hand is raised. It is I. Am I still fated?
Realism is frozen in forgotten ice trays.

"Curled arrows sought by romantic,"
The headline states.
An anxious hammer pounds nails.
I twirl my illusions.
One slips and becomes a dream;
Another, the setting for an artistic rendezvous.
What will she look like?
Will her breasts be full and needing me?
Present-day desires are yesterday's failures.
My eyes close as the room spins.
I feel the rope around my neck.
I feel what being seems to be
Your face, always beyond reach,
Just yonder. What I perceive as close is
You again, you again
And again,
A different face on a sumptuous body.

No, Mother. Never again.
That happens only once.
It is you. Or are you now her?
All females are portrayed by the apple and the prickly pear.
Yoko Ono,
The sear that calmed a storm,
Was hated because love is very dangerous.
The young soldier orders me to stand straight against a wall.
Never waste bullets.
Modern painting is beauty caught in a devil's web.

Back in the crypt
On Rue Morgue,
In the House of Wax,
It is fundamental to be outside yourself,
Looking for a reason to comprehend all the motives.
The seas cling, it lulls reminding me of my loneliness:
Never touching, always longing for,
A wave that becomes a beautiful, twisting ribbon.
The call is unmistakable.
In hindsight, I see that I should have chosen life
Instead of living,
An arrangement of always becoming.
Meandering in a mind obscured by the perpetual performance of thought.
Squeezed by intellect and murdered by mental activity.
With no outlet,
My emotions fracture. Blood drops ooze.
All of my gray matter decompresses,
Shocked between genius and madness.
There is no refection,
Just a mirror, or a memory, of one.

(Brahms Violin Concerto No. 1 plays.)

The Jury Returns

What is the background for this expressive grief?
Salsa plays against "Moonlight Serenade."
In the executioner's chair,
I am reminded that I did not fulfill the wishes of my father.
I sip red wine, eat spaghetti, and scowl at the guards.
In the sight of every criminal, I crawl to uplift my ego.
Then the armed cavaliers storm the toilets, flushing us under the ice.
Like landslides separating the glistening from the ethereal,
The eventful, opinionated dream begins.
I am all the players. I sit and sneer at all the I's who think they are me.
All of us are naked in silk suits with open-collar shirts.
Rings, bracelets, watches, and neck chains—
Those wearing fish net panty hose bang at my dressing-room door.
In a fool's outfit, I loosen the reins of present-day incompetence.
Church bells ring, bringing a chill
To the moneylenders who are afraid of the Second Coming.
A curtain is drawn.
Duke Pearson takes the stage
Newspaper swallows promote a Moroccan war.
Every backyard must have a statue
Penelope seducing Calypso
Winding a clock backward.
Poems dismantle
Silenced time.
Homer is brought before the courts
To defend Shakespeare's interpretation of psychological intervention.
I just laugh,
Continuing a slow dance with Helen.
She will not sleep with me, so I engage another prostitute.

At the point where perpendiculars intersect with tears from Russian plays,
I erase myself from the portraits.
It is winter,
With many stoic paintings of gilded crucifixions.
I look to Achilles
To give me the signal to move on.

As the guests arrive, I conquer what any death leaves behind.
Troubled by this tortured mind with many voices
Large and small,
This delinquent, the poet and the child, is
Scared, full of self-hatred, and
Smothered from memories long faded.
Understood emotions can never be interpreted.
I find myself once more.
I am inside the marble, but my mind is tracking the sculptor's inspiration.
Locked in what never will be unlocked,
In the dim light of pictorial relevance,
I accept the gloom that shrouds seduction,
Never tempting tomorrow,
Behind the beginning,
With she-devils pillaging my mind.
My brain asks questions only a troubled psychotic can answer.
The glass cracks and shatters,
Then bursts.
Museum collectors of abstract "I" find me in bedrooms, absent from myself,
Alive yet dead—but alive.
They know that I knew that
All that is fixed in time has no consequence to the mind.

The drinking continues.
The redhead, the blonde, the brunette,
And the silver-haired lady all stand nude before me,
But I am encased in honey colored vinyl. I can reach out but never touch.
Cranes spread their wings. Without knowing that oceans persist,
I am distant,
Stained in sin,
Bathed in snares, and denied admission.
Merciless.
As the composition nears completion,
I discern that destruction is the course.
Like a galloping thoroughbred,
Enchantment gores.

The intrigue is in the thought a second before the consciousness
Casts any perspective
Across the landscape of the lifeless.
A rusty hook drags.
What is unconceivable?
My birth.

Debussy composes the ocean.
Caravaggio examines the perspective.
Jesus and Isadora Duncan fondle Joan of Arc.
God flicks his cigarette at me and smirks.
"Commit suicide once more and we'll speak."
Garbled voices entwine, hissing the word *never.*
The hard bargaining begins.
Souls and the queen of hearts.
Modern music and modern art.
Postpartum compositions created without direction.
Though the relationships are deleted, memories of the pain remain,
Linger with unrestrained contrition and
In silence
As the words,
I-love-you, are recalled.
Only madness accompanies thoughts that are cursed to separate and introspect.
Eliminate all that is impossible
And you find that what remains is thought.

Maybe a razor—maybe a blade.
Maybe
Existence dismissing life.
Maybe
I will be mine,
Free from pain
Forever,
Deeply in love.
The white whale has begun his charge.
Surrealism's journey continues.
The distress signal sounds.

The wooden horse.
The evolving self.
Shattering busts of Apollinaire.

(Refrain from Brahms Violin Concerto No. 1 plays.)

Is that you?
Unyielding, I hear her
Coming to me.
The stinging from the black leather whip.
Once,
Twice,
And again.
My eyes widening,
Widening
In the cold vastness,
As a glowing
Hot branding iron
Is about to touch my heart.
"Kyrie eleison."
"Christe eleison."
"Kyrie eleison."

A voice trapped inside my head forever.

You should be dead
You should be dead
You should be dead
You should be dead
You should be dead
You should be dead
You should be dead
You should be dead
You should be dead
You should be dead
You should be dead
You should be dead
You should be dead

Most of all, I miss you so.
Most of all, I miss you so.
Most of all, I miss you so.

by Russian/Italian artist Tomaeva-Gabellini Fatima

ON OPENING NIGHT, THE CAST WAVE GOOD-BYE AS I CHART A COURSE TO RETURN

"Vexed,"
she said.
I thought,
What a wonderful word.
Therefore, I looked it up.
I found its meaning.
Yes, I am annoying.
Of course, I did not look it up.
This was all in my mind.
I was lying with my eyes closed,
Waiting for the phone to ring,
Thinking of ways
To exempt myself from life.

Curiously,
She could not recognize love,
Not once more.
To sleep without chaos.
She was not naive.
Her ideas disassembled.
I perceived the horrors
When the young girl gave me
An urn full of ashes.
The other,
Who always relied on the kindness of strangers,
Had hidden herself
From people and their requests.

The landscape prevails.
I arrive on the shore
On a moonless night,
Waiting for dawn
To follow my footsteps.
Heaven's customs never vary.
Since I sailed the seas,
I have broken every commandment.
The wind carries many scents.
I choose the smell of you, of her, and of the others.
Loneliness is woven into my thoughts.
The wall of incomprehensibility
Begins to crumble from expectation.

Mysticism roots into my mind and
Delivers diversions,
Like lakes holding hostages.
Small boats remain afloat in storms.
Now the journey has come full circle.
I am home, or I think so.
Colliding memories bring me forward
Until remorse drags me back.
No coastal glaciers can cool me.
The die is cast.
More definite than beautiful,
I collect myself
In a singular thought.

Mountains see misfortune.
They trace my outline.
I am punished and forgotten.
Yesterday, when I left, I was
Gallant and impressionable,
At the behest of the goddesses.
Rich in voice and with little comfort,
From home to adventures,

In beds of gold with cold deliverers,
I am now coming back to you,
My mind wet with experience, knowledge,
And superior watchfulness
Regarding what ambitions I have left.

My love is true.
The journey is irretrievable,
All afterglows now.
Whirlpools collect
Images of you
Back from before your
Legs were spread,
Your breasts heavy.
Exploring our possessions.
Crossroads in your mind.
Thunderous suitors
Interpreting adornments,
Illuminating my way.

They say that apologies
Unlock hearts.
Grateful for homecomings, I wonder,
Was anything ever mine?
Rummaging through disasters,
Unwanted for being,
Loved for excesses.
The bell tolls,
Reminding us all that
Life is always fetching.
The seclusion of swimming.
Doomed fleeting moments.
Always another inflamed eternity.

Self-flagellating
Against love.

Tormented by the gods.
Insisting on mutilation,
Fantasizing I am
The rapture your heart desires,
I have an array of daggers,
One for every instance,
Whether blue, brown, or green eyes.
Opposing voyages race
To empty every emotion.
I am always solitary,
Escaping death's throes.

Achilles never enjoyed my company.
Ulysses was always preoccupied.
Hector and Paris thought me irrelevant.
Helen was too young
Penelope had only one love.
Calypso needed men of strength.
Circe calculated with cunning.
The men chased the wind.
Sirens preferred each other.
God laughs at failure.
Contemptuous of myself,
I sit at the bar,
Composing my adventure.

I wore an English-cut suit and
Walked to 221B Baker Street.
A tall, thin male figure greeted me.
He said, "I've been expecting you."
I answered, "Can you find it—
The fabric of my mind?"
"Yes, my good fellow. I already have," he said.
There is no reality, just logic.
I stared at my fictional idol.

He continued. "The improbable prevails."
I look into a large Victorian mirror. There I am.
He very gracefully hands me a book, saying, "Ah, here you are."
The book's title? *Dark Images at Sea.*

Photograph by Scottish photographer Stuart McAllister – Effects by German photographer Jens Neubauer

Printed in the United States
By Bookmasters